WOMEN IN FAMILY DECISION MAKING

By

Dr. Edwin Gnanadhas
M.Com, M.Phil, Ph.D.
Reader of Commerce
Scott Christian College
Nagerccoil
(Tamilnadu)

&

Dr. Chithra James
M.Com, M.Phil, Ph.D.
Lecturer in Commerce
Women's Christian College
Nagerccoil
(Tamilnadu)

DISCOVERY PUBLISHING HOUSE PVT. LTD.
NEW DELHI-110 002

Published by:
Tilak Wasan

DISCOVERY PUBLISHING HOUSE PVT. LTD.
4831/24, Ansari Road, Prahlad Street
Darya Ganj, New Delhi-110002 (India)
Phone: +91-11-23279245, 43764432
Fax: +91-11-23253475
E-mail: parul.wasan@gmail.com
discoverypublishinghouse@gmail.com
info@discoverypublishinggroup.com
web: www.discoverypublishinggroup.com

First Edition: **2011**
ISBN: 978-81-8356-747-3

Printed at:
Shree Balaji Art Press
Delhi

Preface

The decision making power in the hands of a woman is not only a symbol of her status but also an indicator of modern society. It ultimately benefits the household, the society and the economy as a whole. Working women's affluence, independence and self confidence in 'modern women' have created a substantial change in the women's purchasing roles. The increased autonomy of the modern wife implies that she can make some of the decisions that are already made by the husband. Women are increasingly performing tasks traditionally assigned to men. Now women are considered as a pivot around which the family revolves. There is a drastic change of women's role in the recent past especially in a developing country like India. Major shifts in women's role structures should be reflected in the market place. Marketing managers should respond to the changing woman's role through introduction of new products designed to the appeal of the new emerging attitudes and the partial repositioning of existing products and changing advertising strategy.

It is in this context that systematic studies about the women factor in the purchase decision making in the household economy is called for to study the buying behaviour of selected durables, the process of Family Decision Making, the role of Women in Family Purchase Decision and the socio-economic factors influencing women in decision making. This book is a research work which involves lot of effort on the part of the researcher.

This empirical study is organised into seven chapters.

The first chapter deals with the design of the study. It contains the introduction, need for the study, statement of problem, objectives of the study, the scope of the study, the methodology, and the scheme of the report.

The second chapter gives the review of the previous research literature.

The third chapter presents the literature of the process of consumer decision making and the area profile.

The fourth chapter discusses the buying behaviour of the durables selected and the process of family decision making.

The fifth chapter analyses the role of women in family purchase decision making.

The sixth chapter emphasises the final decision makers in the family purchase of durable goods.

The last chapter recapitulates the key findings and conclusion of the study. Based on these findings, a few suggestions have been made for the women to be an effective decision maker in the family and marketers to succeed in this competitive world by designing a good marketing mix.

We are grateful to *Dr. Sinthihiyal, M.A.,Ph.D.,* Principal, Women's Christian College, Nagercoil and *Dr. Chellakumar Rose, M.A., M.Phil., Ph.D.,* Principal, Scott Christian College, Nagercoil for having given me an opportunity to do this and their encouragement and support.

We sincerely thank *Mr. Dennis Guru Sahayam, M.A.,PGDTE., Dip. in J&C,* retired Head of the Department of English, Nesamony Memorial College, Marthandam for the fine editing and shaping of this thesis.

We thank our friends and colleagues for their encouragement and inspiration in all possible ways especially *Dr. Rathiha.* We are thankful to *Dr. Sam Christudhas, M.B.A., Ph.D., and Dr. L Manivannan M.B.A., Ph.D* S.G. Lecturers, Erode Arts College, for their encouragement and help in the course of work.

Dr. Chithra is always indebted to her husband *Mr. W. Joseph Thambi Nayagam* for his gentle understanding, mutual participation and presentable efforts and her sweet child *J. Shekina* for her cheerful smile and tolerance while achieving this research task at the cost of her recreative hours.

Above all we thank Almighty God who is the author of all inspirations.

M.EDWIN GNANADHAS

CHITHRA JAMES

Contents

Preface

1. Introduction 1
2. Review of Literature 24
3. Consumer Decision Making 43
4. Buying Behaviour of Durable Goods 62
5. Role of Women in the Decision-Making Process of Family Purchase 104
6. Final Decison Makers in the Family Purchase of Durable Goods 131
7. Summary of Findings, Suggestions and Conclusion ... 164

Bibliography *179*

Index 187

Introduction

The field of consumer behaviour is rooted in a marketing strategy that evolved in the late 1950's when marketers began to realise that they could sell more goods more easily, if they produced only those goods that the consumer had determined to buy. Instead of trying to persuade the consumers to buy what the firm has already produced, marketing-oriented firms have found that it is easier to produce only products that would satisfy the needs of the customers. Through consumer research it is found out that consumers purchase impulsively and are also influenced by the family, advertisers and role models besides by the mood, situation and emotion.[1] All of these factors combine to form a comprehensive model of consumer behaviour that reflects both the cognitive and emotional aspects of consumer decision making. This study is based on one of the external influences of consumer decision making *i.e.,* the family.

Family plays an important role in purchase decisions as it is a natural buying unit in the society. Family is both a primary group characterised by intimate and face to face interaction and a reference group with members referring to certain family values, norms and standards in their behaviour. The bonds within the family are likely to be more powerful than those in other groups and contrary to most other groups, the family functions directly in the role of ultimate consumption. Thus the family operates as an economic unit, earning and spending money. In doing this, the members of the family must establish individual and collective consumption priorities, decide on products and brands that fulfill their needs and also finalise from where these items are to be bought and how they are to be used in furthering the goals of the family members. Consumer's attitude towards spending, saving and choosing the brands and stores and the purchase of products have been moulded by the family environment they grow up in. Thus marketers need to understand the nature of the family's influence on its members and the way in which purchase decisions are made by members so that they can effectively programme their marketing mix.

Women are, universally and traditionally, responsible for caring of children and other members of the household and for all the domestic work that their caring roles entitle. They often have primary responsibilities for the health of all the members of the family, provision of food, water and fuel. But men in the family are considered as providers or breadwinners.

Despite several efforts, a woman in Indian society is still considered inferior to man and she does not have an independent identity. Both in North and South India, among all religions, the family is mainly patriarchal, patrilocal and patrileneal, and India has long been known for inequalitarian gender relations (Jeejeeboy, 2002)[2]. Women are defined as inferior and husbands are assumed to 'own' women and have the right to dominate them. In this situation of generally limited autonomy, sharp cultural and regional differences are found in Indian women.

Women in India are playing a significant role in the mainstream of the economy as well as in the domestic labour sector. Over 118 million women are reported to be active members of the workforce in the Indian economy as workers in the informal economy, farm workers, casual workers, domestic helpers, piece-rate workers for garment and other craft and non-craft based small scale industries and workers in the construction industry. Their role as providers and home makers at one end of the socio-economic spectrum, especially rural, has always been known in India but it has to be examined in terms of role in household purchase decisions to fully gauge their impact on business.[3]

Nearly 77 per cent of the women workforce are from the rural sector engaged in agriculture and agri-produce based small/cottage enterprises often with part time and multi industry engagement but there are no fixed employment or fixed income patterns. Thus their earnings as well as their role in spending needs to be closely examined. On the other hand, nearly 10 per cent of this workforce of women is engaged in the manufacturing sector that is more organised. Further in the urban educated workforce of women, their role in decisions regarding family spending is more well known now as they are actively engaged in the role in deciding what items are to be purchased and the brand.[4]

In the recent past there have been significant changes in terms of consumption which has reflected in their role in decision-making regarding lifestyles and in determining the roles of various members of the family in consumption. Economic dependence, improvement in education and awareness, work oriented lifestyles, changing social norms, increased participation in the workforce and a society more open to change have led to an enhancement in the role of women in the family consumption related decision-making process. Women today are more independent in their thinking and financially also. They are the decision makers because they have gained the economic and emotional freedom. Now families are not only supporting her but also accepting her identity (Bajpai 2008).[5] The government's new policy of providing microfinance through self help groups has enabled women in household decision making processes. According to Women Empowerment Project conducted by Opportunities, an NGO, 60 per cent of women have greater power over family planning, buying and selling property and sending their children to school (Verma 2008).[6]

Empowering women is a pre-requisite for creating a

prosperous nation. When women are empowered, society with stability is assured. Empowerment of women is essential as their thoughts and their value systems lead to the development of a good family, society and ultimately a good nation (Abdul Kalam A.P.J).[7]

Women's empowerment in a family includes the women's place or position in terms of making decisions about one's private concerns. Women's status is the degree of women's access to and control over material resources and social resources within the family, in the community and in the society at large (Masan, 1986).[8] Family decision making is the process by which decisions that directly or indirectly involve two or more family members are made. The processes that families use to make purchase decisions and the outcome of these processes have important effects on the well being of the individual family members and the family itself.

Roles of Family Members in the Family Decision Making Process

Family decision making involves consideration of questions such as who buys, who decides and who uses. Family decision making is complex as it involves emotion, interpersonal relations, product evaluation and acquisition. Marketing managers must analyse the household decision process separately for each product category within each target market. The participation in the decision process by a family member depends on his involvement with the specific product, role specialisation, personal characteristics and finally culture and sub culture.

Husband-Wife Decisions

As a consumption unit, the family or household functions like any other group with problems to be solved and decisions to be made. Each member, including children, plays a role, some more active than others. The husband and wife relationship is of key importance to marketers. In order to target their messages effectively, marketers must identify the primary source of influence and the decision maker in each purchase decision made by the husband-wife team. Purchase decisions are divided into four categories (Davis and Rigaux, 1974).[9]

1. Husband dominant family decision making.
2. Wife dominant family decision making.
3. Autonomy in family decision making—husband and wife independently make the same decision taking about one-half of the time.
4. Syncratic family decision making—both husband and wife share in the decision making.

Decision Influencing Factors

Household influence is defined as the degree to which husbands and wives attempt to dominate household decisions (Qualls 1987).[10] The relative influence of the husband and wife may vary according to the type of product, nature of product influence, family characteristics and changing patterns of husband-wife influence.

Type of Product: Husband-wife involvement in family decision making varies widely by product category (Davis, 1976)[11]. Husband dominant decisions have occurred with the purchase of automobiles (Davis 1970,[12] Green and Cunningham, 1975[13]), life insurance (Davis and Rigaux, 1974[14]) and lawn mower (Arora and Allenby, 1999).[15]

Wives have been viewed as the prime decision makers for groceries, kitchen appliances (Green and Cunningham 1975)[16] food, their clothing (Davis and Rigaux, 1974)[17] and microoven (Arora and Allenby, 1999).[18]

Joint decisions are most likely when buying a home (Munsinguer *et al.,* 1975),[19] furniture (Green and Cunningham 1975)[20] and planning a vacation (Davis and Rigaux, 1974).[21]

Most studies have ignored the influence of children (Spiro, 1983).[22] However, children, particularly adolescents, often exert a substantial influence on family decision machine in the purchase of two wheeler (Mohanram and Mahavi, 2007),[23] toothpaste and their clothes (Foxman et al., 1989).[24]

Many of these roles have been merged and even reversed due to the increase in the proportion of working wives and changes in family norms.

These classifications have considerable implications for marketers. If a product is husband-dominant or wife-dominant, marketers must tailor messages to one spouse or the other and must select the media that are male or female dominant. If the product is in the joint decision category, marketers must tailor the message to the taste of the couple and must select the media that are likely to reach both spouses. If there is no specific criteria, marketers may need two campaigns—one directed to the wife and the other to the husband using different appeals.

Nature of Purchase Influence: The nature of the purchase influence may specify husband-wife roles. The purchase influence may be classified as instrumental versus expressive roles in family purchasing. Instrumental roles are related to performing tasks that help the group make the final purchasing decisions. Decisions on budgets, timing and product specifications would be task oriented. Expressive roles facilitate expression of group norms and provide the group with social and emotional support. Decisions about colour, style and design are expressive since they reflect group norms.

Historically the husband has been associated with the instrumental role and the wife with the expressive role (Davis and Rigaux 1974,[25] Hempel 1974,[26] Hansen 1975[27]). However as more wives enter the working sector, husbands are more likely to assume household roles and wives budgetary and planning roles. Thus these two roles can be exchanged between the husband and the wife. Ferber and Lee (1974)[28] suggest that the wife may be just as likely as the husband to fulfill certain instrumental roles. They have identified the role of the family financial officer who pays the bills, keeps track of expenditure and determines the cash that is left.

Family Characteristics: Even though husbands tend to dominate decisions for certain product categories and wives for others, these roles may vary in the degree of dominance within each family. In patriarchal families, the husband may be more dominant regardless of the product and in matriarchal families, the wife more dominant.

A profile of the husband dominant family suggests a family with traditional values and attitudes toward marital roles (Green and Cunningham 1975).[29] A husband's higher income provides him with financial power within the family. When there is a non-working wife with a lower level of education more traditional values prevail in the family.

In another study wives are classified as conservative, moderate or liberal with regard to female roles (Green and Cunningham 1975).[30] Women who have liberal views are much more likely to make purchase decisions than low conservative women. Conversely, a study of husbands has found that those with conservative perceptions of their marital roles believe that they have more influence on vacations, insurance and savings than the husbands with more liberal views (Qualls, 1987).[31]

Changing Patterns of Husband-Wife Influence: Changes in marital roles have led to the husband's greater influence in decisions that the wife has traditionally assumed and the wife's greater influence in areas that are traditionally assumed to be the husbands domain (Green and Cuningham, 1975).[32]

Children's Influence on Decisions

Adolescents have a number of strategies which they use in interacting with their parents when participating in family decision making (Palan and Wikes 1994).[33] They bargain, trying to create agreement based on mutual gain. They persuade and convince opposing family members to resolve the conflict in the teen's favour. They may use emotion laden tactics including crying, withdrawing, pouting, anger or remain silent in order to get their way (Spiro 1983).[34] Children inspired by television advertising and peer pressure among school friends, plead, whine and bargain with their parents to get what they want (Isler, 1987).[35]

The factors that have been found to impact children's degree of influence in family decision making are:

(*i*) Product Type: Children frequently accompany parents to super markets and influence grocery shopping and brand choices to a great extent depending upon the product purchased. The greatest number of attempts to influence and the highest number of incidents of parental yielding occur, predictably in the product categories of breakfast cereal, snacks, candy, soft drinks, games and toys (Ward and Wackman 1972).[36]

(*ii*) Children's Personal Resources: Children's personal resources include their income, employment status, school grades, birth order, and parents' love and confidence. The more personal resources the child has, the greater is his influence in family purchase decisions (Foxman *et al.*, 1989).[37]

(*iii*) Children's Age: Children's attempts to influence tend to increase with age and mothers are more willing to yield to such children. Older children have more experience with products and have learned more about consumer roles. They are much more likely to be consulted by parents in major purchase decisions. Teens as they take on more household purchases, exert a strong influence over buying decisions.

(*iv*) Mothers' Child-centeredness: One study of mother's choices in cereals has reported that more child-centered mothers do not give in to their child's preferences as much as mothers who are less child-centered (Berey and Pollay, 1968).[38]

(*v*) Family Communication Environment: There are two styles of communication within families. Socio-oriented communication is characterised by harmony, pleasant and social interactions and avoidance of conflict and controversy. But concept-oriented communication reflects individual thought and analysis. Children in socio-oriented families have limited influence on purchases and are expected to go along with parents decisions. Those from concept-oriented families exert greater influence as they are encouraged to think and evaluate options on their own (Moschis, 1985).[39]

(*vi*) Parental Style: There are three styles of parenting. Authoritarian parents restrict their children's activities instead of nurturing. Authoritative parents set limits, but encourage them. Permissive parents nurture the children's activities but do not set restrictions. The influence of children tends to be highest in families with permissive parents, followed by families with authoritative parents and is low in families with authoritarian parents (Carlson and Grossbart 1988).[40]

Need for the Study

The decision-making power in the hands of a woman is not only a symbol of her status but also an indicator of modern society. It ultimately benefits the household, the society and the economy as a whole. Working women's affluence, independence and self confidence in 'modern women' have created a substantial change in the women's purchasing roles. The increased autonomy of the modern wife implies that she can make some of the decisions that are already made by the husband. Women are increasingly performing tasks traditionally assigned to men. Now women are considered as a pivot around which the family revolves. There is a drastic change of women's role in the recent past especially in a developing country like India. Major shifts in women's role structures should be reflected in the market place. Marketing managers should respond to the changing woman's role through introduction of new products designed to the appeal of the new emerging attitudes and the partial repositioning of existing products and changing advertising strategy.

It is in this context that systematic studies about the women factor in the purchase decision-making in the household economy is called for.

Statement of the Problem

Marketing communication builds on marketer's knowledge of how consumers make decisions in families. In particular, marketers are interested in understanding spousal influence patterns and decision processes in order to target communication messages. To persuade couples effectively to choose a particular brand, a marketer has to know which spouse has primary influence in the purchase decision for the product category. This knowledge may enable a marketer to target communications more accurately. Thus an effective promotional programme should build on family decision dynamic to communicate differentiated marketing messages to the right influential spouses who take the decisions.

Besides, only a few studies have been made with regard to women consumers, especially in India. This study is an attempt to bridge the gap in this regard.

Democratic and secular India endeavours to provide the necessary conditions for greater participation of women in all spheres of life. Equality in opportunity is guaranteed and discrimination on grounds of sex, language, region, class or creed is prohibited. However, in reality, women's participation in decision-making at all levels—national or local—is low. The challenges in seeking to redress this inequality in a diverse and complex country like India are enormous.

As women constitute half the population, women must be associated in decision-making in all socio-economic and political organisations. Obstacles which do not let women to participate need to be identified and removed. Often structures and social norms are barriers and stem from social conditions which inhibit women from aspiring to decision making positions. Governmental and non-governmental interventions should facilitate and promote women's participation in decision making.

In India, even in the privacy of a home, men and women seem to be keeping decision making gender-based. Women voicing their feelings, dissent or preferences are exceptions. Women assume leadership positions and be successful if they are enabled to develop their confidence right from the childhood and not just after marriage as a wife. Unless their lives are made more conductive and more empowered within the institution of the family, the chances of their reaching all that is promised to them in government policies and plans will remain only on paper.

It is, therefore, required a study like this to investigate, understand and analyse their problems relating to their low profile, the nature of some cultural and institutional barriers that hinder their effective participation in the decision-making at all levels.

The extent to which women's voices are heard within the family also varies widely by customs, culture and region. Culturally, south Indian women are enjoying a higher status than those in North India. They are considerably better off in freedom to choose education and an occupation.

Therefore, the problem selected for the study is "The 'women' factor in family purchase decisions—A study with reference to selected durables".

Scope of the Study

The present study is conducted in every phase in the family decision making process and the role of women starting from the need recognition to the search, evaluation of product alternatives and in deciding the product features and store of purchase and the post purchase behaviour of family members in the purchase of Television, Refrigerator, Washing Machine and Two Wheeler. Understanding the role of women in family purchase decision making is an interesting as well as a very important area of study in this changing economy.

In advanced countries considerable research work has

been done. As only very few Indian research works are available on the present topic, there is wider scope to study the same.

Objectives of the Study

The main objective of the study is to examine the 'women' factor in the family purchase decisions of Television, Refrigerator, Washing Machine and Two Wheeler.

The specific objectives of the study are:

1. To study the buying behaviour of women especially with regard to the selected durable goods in the study.
2. To investigate the purchase process of durable goods in the family.
3. To ascertain the factors that influence women in purchase decisions of selected durable goods.
4. To find out the role of women in the family on purchase decision of durable goods.
5. To study the influence of women socio-economic factor in the purchase of durable goods.

Null Hypothesis Defined

Ho_1: There is no significant relationship between rural and urban families and the role of members in family decision making.

Ho_2: There is no significant association between working and non working women and the role of members in family decision making.

Ho_3: There is no relationship between demographic factors and women as family purchase decision makers.

Operational Definitions

Autonomy

It is the ability to obtain information and to use it as the basis for making decisions about one's private concerns and one's intimates.

Durable Goods

Goods that are not consumed or disposed of quickly but have a shelf life of more than three years are called durable goods or hard goods.

Empower

To empower is to give somebody the power or authority to do something or to give somebody better control over his/her own life or the situation he/she is in.

Extended Family

The nuclear family together with atleast one grand parent living within the household is called an extended or joint family.

Family

A family is a group of two people or more related by birth, marriage or adoption and residing together.

Family Decision Making

It is the process by which decisions that directly or indirectly involve two or more family members are made.

Family Purchase Decisions

It is the decision taken by the family member or members in the purchase of goods or service.

Nuclear Family

A husband and wife and one or more children constitute a nuclear family.

Selected Durables

The word 'selected durables' includes Television, Refrigerator, Washing Machine and Two Wheeler. Only these four durables are studied in detail in this study even though data are collected about other durables to study the consumer behaviour.

Women

In this study the 'women' factor includes only married women above the age of 21 and below the age of 60 who are living with their husband with or without their child/ children. Divorced and separated women and widows are not considered for the purpose of this study.

Methodology

The present study is an empirical study based on survey method. The primary data is collected with the help of a pre-tested and well-structured questionnaire from 355 women covering urban and rural areas and working and non-working respondents.

Secondary data pertaining to this research are collected from Statistical Hand Books and other books, journals, records and websites.

Construction of Questionnaire

The questionnaire schedule employed in this study is constructed carefully by the researcher with the help of the supervisor. In order to test the validity of the format, and for evaluation it has been presented to research experts in the field of social sciences.

The variables of the study are identified by referring to various research reports and articles and used to design the questionnaire. Afterwards the rough draft has been prepared and pilot study conducted with 40 women respondents. Keeping in mind, the suggestions of experts and comments of the pre-tested respondents, the rough draft has been revised and the final draft prepared and used for collecting data.

The questionnaire consists of two parts. The first part contains the demographic information in order to know and understand the profile of the respondents. The second part includes the questions regarding the consumer behaviour and the family decision making process.

Durables Selected for the Study

In order to explore the role of women in family purchase decisions, four consumer durables have been selected namely Television, Refrigerator, Washing Machine and Two Wheeler. The selection of these four durables and the techniques used to measure marital roles can be identified because these four purchases of durable goods represent important family decisions. Also they usually involve substantial financial outlay, extended period of ownership, social importance and joint use by all the members of the family. Hence, all the family members are expected to participate in one way or other in making decisions.

Sampling Technique

For the purpose of this study the data have been collected from married women. For the selection of women respondents Non-Probability Convenient Sampling Technique has been adopted as it well suits exploratory studies like this (Singh and Kaur, 2004).[41] However due care is taken to include women with various socio-economic background to make the sample representative. The size of the sample is 355 women respondents.

Data Processing

After completing the collection of data collection with the help of questionnaire method a thorough verification has been made for further processing of data. Proper editing work is made wherever necessary. Next each question is coded and fed into the computer with the help of SPSS package for further analysis. At the time of processing the data, 45 questionnaires have been rejected as they lacked completeness and accuracy.

Framework of Analysis

Various mathematical and statistical tools have been used for analysing the data collected for the study.

(*i*) "Henry's Garrett Ranking Technique" is used to rank the reasons for purchasing durables, to know the most inducement factor for the purchase of durables and to find out the reasons for store selection in the purchase of durables.

The percentage position is determined with the help of the following formula

$$\text{Percentage Position} = \frac{100(R_{ij} - 0.5)}{N}$$

Where,

R = Rank assigned for the variables by the respondents

N = Number of statements ranked by the respondents

Mean score is obtained with the help of the following formula

$$\text{Mean Score} = \frac{\Sigma fx}{N}$$

fx = Total Score

N = Number of Respondents

(ii) "Factor Analysis" is used to reduce and group the factors influencing the purchase of selected durable goods.

The technique of factor analysis provides a fascinating way of reducing the number of variables by combining related ones into factors. For the purpose of extracting factors, 'Principal Component Analysis' has been used. In this study all the factors with an Eigen Value of 1 or more is extracted.

Then, in order to assign variables to factors and to interpret them the 'Rotated Factor Matrix' has been used.

The Factor Analysis Model in Matrix rotation is

$$x = \text{Af} + \text{e}$$

Where $x = [x_1 + x_2 + x_3 + \ldots\ldots\ldots\ldots + x_p]$

$$f = [f_1 + f_2 + f_3 + ... + f_m]$$
$$e = [e_1 + e_2 + e_3 + ... + e_p]$$
$$m = \text{Number of factors}$$
$$p = \text{Number of variables}$$

This Rotated Factor Matrix is viewed column-wise and the variables which have higher loadings are identified and a combined meaning for the factor is given. These factors can be used to design communication and marketing strategies.

In this study, Factor Analysis is also used to identify the factors for the dominance of husband or wife in the family purchase decisions. Factor Analysis is used after testing its appropriateness with the help of Kaiser Meyer Olkin (KMO) test and Bartlett's test.

(iii) Chi-square test is applied to test the hypothesis (Ho_1 and Ho_2) of finding out the association between demographic factors of area of residence and women's employment and role of members in family decision making.

The formula for chi-square is

$$\chi^2 = S[(O - E)^2/E]$$
$$E = \frac{RT \times CT}{N}$$
$$E = \text{Expected frequency}$$
$$RT = \text{The row total}$$
$$CT = \text{The column total}$$
$$N = \text{The total number of observation}$$
$$v = (c - 1)(r - 1)$$
$$v = \text{number of degrees of freedom}$$

(iv) In order to test the hypothesis (Ho_3) of the relationship between demographic factors and women in family purchase decision making Analysis of Variance (ANOVA) has been employed.

The Analysis of Variance technique developed by R.A. Fisher in 1920's is calculated with the help of the following formula.

$$F = \frac{\text{Variance between samples}}{\text{Variance within samples}}$$

$$F - \text{ratio} = \frac{\text{Mean Squares (MS) between}}{\text{Mean Squares (MS) within}}$$

Where,

$$\text{MS between} = \frac{\text{Sum of Squares (SS) between}}{(k-1)}$$

$$\text{MS within} = \frac{\text{Sum of Squares (SS) within}}{(n-k)}$$

and k = number of samples

n = Total number of items in all the samples

(v) Multiple Linear Regression Analysis is used to explain the dependent variables of purchase decision made by women based on the variation of eleven independent variables.

A regression is a statistical tool used to explain the variation of one dependent variable based on the variation in one or more independent variables. If there is only one Dependent Variable and one Independent Variable used to explain the variation in it, it is a simple regression. If multiple independent variable are used to explain the variation in a dependent variable it is called a Multiple Regression Model.

The general Multiple Linear Regression Model is

$$y = a + b_1x_1 + b_2x_2 + \ldots\ldots + b_nx_n$$

Where y is the dependent variable and $x_1, x_2 \ldots x_n$ are the independent variables expected to be related to y and expected to predict y. $b_1, b_2 \ldots b_n$ are the co-efficients of the respective independent variables. 'a' is a constant.

(vi) Multiple Discriminant Analysis is used in this study to discriminate the high and the low level of women in family decision making.

The objective of Multi Discriminant Analysis is to predict an object's likelihood of belonging to a particular group based on several independent variables. The Multi Discriminant Analysis reveals the specific variables to account for the largest proportion of inter-group differences. It is a simple scoring system that assigns a score to each individual or object. This score is a weighted average of the individual's numerical value of the independent variables. The individual is assigned the 'most likely' category on the basis of this score. The model is represented as,

$$Z_i = \beta_0 + \beta_1 X_{il} + ... + \beta_j X_{ik}$$

Where X_{ik} is the ith individual's value of the kth independent variable, β_j is the multiple discriminant coefficient of the kth variable. Z_i is the ith individual's multiple discriminant score.

(*vii*) To find out the most and least important factors influencing the purchase of selected durables, "Likerts Five Point Scaling Technique" is adopted.

Period of Study

The present study is aimed at studying the 'women' factor in family purchase decision for the purchase of Television, Refrigerator, Washing Machine and Two Wheeler. So data have been collected from women who own all these four durable goods during the period from August '07 to January '08.

Limitations of the Study

1. The data presented in this study represent the view of women only as wives. It may not be totally accurate with respect to actual family decision making patterns.
2. A second limitation involves the possibility that in many cases decisions concerning the goods used in the study might not have been made in the recent past. Thus a portion of the sample is probably responding hypothetically with regard to the goods rather than on the basis of recent experience.

3. The present study is a post-hoc analysis of decision making. Therefore, actual decision-making has not been observed, rather it is reported.
4. Although the roles of children and the husband have been enquired, their individual responses are not measured.

Chapter Scheme

This empirical study is organised into seven chapters:

The *first* chapter deals with the design of the study. It contains the introduction, need for the study, statement of problem, objectives of the study, the scope of the study, the methodology, and the scheme of the report.

The *second* chapter gives the review of the previous research literature.

The *third* chapter presents the literature of the process of consumer decision making and the area profile.

The *fourth* chapter discusses the buying behaviour of the durables selected and the process of family decision making.

The *fifth* chapter analyses the role of women in family purchase decision making.

The *sixth* chapter emphasises the final decision makers in the family purchase of durable goods.

The *Seventh* chapter recapitulates the key findings and conclusion of the study. Based on these findings, a few suggestions have been made for the women to be an effective decision maker in the family and marketers to succeed in this competitive world by designing a good marketing mix.

REFERENCES

1. Leon G. Schiffman et al., *Consumer Behaviour*, Prentice-Hall of India Private Limited, New Delhi, 2005, p. 19.
2. Shireen T. Jejeebhoy, "Convergence and Divergence in Spouses Perspectives on Women's Autonomy in Rural India", *Studies in Family Planning*, Vol.33, No.4, December 2002, pp. 299-308.

3. Hawkins et al., "Consumer Behaviour Building Marketing Strategy", Ninth Edition, Tata McGraw Hill Publishing Company Limited, New Delhi, 2007, p. 49.
4. Ibid.
5. Suman Bajpai, "Women is Becoming Techno-Smart", *Woman's Era*, Vol.35, No.828, June (first) 2008, pp. 12-14.
6. Renu Verma, "Microfinance and Empowerment of Rural Women", *Kurukshetra*, Vol.56, No.11, September 2008, pp. 3-5.
7. Former Indian President Dr. Abdul Kalam A.P.J., Quoted in Roy S.C., *Legal Empowerment of Women*, p. 735.
8. Masan, K., "The Status of Women; Conceptual and Methodological Issues in Demographic Studies", *Sociological Forum* 1 (2); pp. 284-300.
9. Harry L. Davis and Benny P. Rigaux, "Perception of Marital Roles in Decision Processes", *Journal of Consumer Research*, Vol.1, No.1, June 1974, pp. 51-62.
10. William J. Qualls, "Household Decision Behaviour: The Impact of Husbands' and Wives' Sex Role Orientation", *Journal of Consumer Research*, Vol.14, No.4, September 1987, pp. 264-279.
11. Harry L. Davis, "Decision Making Within the Household", *Journal of Consumer Research*, Vol.2, No.4, March 1976, pp.241-260.
12. Harry L. Davis, "Dimensions of Marital Roles in Consumer Decision Making", *Journal of Marketing Research*, Vol.VII, No. 2, May 1970, pp. 168-77.
13. Robert T. Green and Isabella Cunningham, C.M., "Feminine Role Perception and Family Purchasing Decision", *Journal of Marketing Research*, Vol.XII, No.3, August 1975, pp. 325-32.
14. Harry L. Davis and Benny P. Rigaux, *op.cit*., pp. 51-62.
15. Neeraj Arora and Greg M. Allenby, "Measuring the Influence of Individual Preference Structures in Group Decision Making", *Journal of Marketing Research*, Vol.XXXVI, No.4, November 1999, pp. 476-487.
16. Robert T. Green and Isabella Cunningham, C.M., *op.cit* ., pp. 325-32.
17. Harry L. Davis and Benny P. Rigaux, *op.cit*., pp. 51-62.
18. Neeraj Arora and Greg M. Allenby, *op.cit*., pp. 476-487.
19. Gary M. Munsinguer, Jean E. Weber and Richard W. Hansen, "Joint Home Purchasing Decisions by Husbands and Wives", *Journal of Consumer Research*, Vol.1, No.4, March 1975, pp. 60-66.

20. Robert T. Green and Isabella Cunningham, *op.cit.*, pp.325-32.
21. Harry L. Davis and Benny P. Rigaux, *op.cit.*, pp.51-62.
22. Rosann L. Spiro, "Persuasion in Family Decision-Making", *Journal of Consumer Research*, Vol.9, No.4, March 1983, pp. 393-402.
23. Mohanram, A.S., and Mahavi, C., "Product Related Characteristics, Promotion and Marketing Mix are Key Tools in Determining Purchase Behaviour and Purchase Decision by Teenagers—An Empirical Study", *Indian Journal of Marketing*, Vol. XXXVII, No. 2, February 2007, p. 3-12.
24. Ellen R. Foxman, Patriya S. Tansuhaj and Karin M. Ekstrom, "Family Member's Perceptions of Adolescents' Influence in Family Decision Making', *Journal of Consumer Research*, Vol. 15, No.4, March 1989, pp. 482-491.
25. Harry L. Davis and Benny P. Rigaux, *op.cit.*, pp. 51-62.
26. Donald J. Hempel, "Family Buying Decisions: A Cross Cultural Perspective", *Journal of Marketing Research*, Vol. XI, No. 3, August 1974, pp. 295-302.
27. Gary M. Munsinger, Jean E. Weber and Richard W. Hansen, *op.cit.*, pp. 60-66.
28. Robert Ferber and Lucy Chao Lee, "Husband-Wife Influence in Family Purchasing Behaviour", *Journal of Consumer Research*, Vol.1, No.2, June 1974, pp.43-50.
29. Robert T. Green and Isabella Cunningham, C.M., *op.cit.*, pp. 325-32.
30. *Ibid.*
31. William J. Qualls, *op.cit.*, pp. 264-279.
32. Robert T. Green and Isabella Cunningham, C.M., *op.cit.*, pp. 325-32.
33. Kay N. Palan and Robert E. Wilkes, "Adolescent-Parent Interaction in Family Decision Making", *Journal of Consumer Research*, Vol.24, No.2, September 1997, pp. 159-169.
34. Rasann L. Spiro, "Persuasion in Family Decision Making", *Journal of Consumer Research*, Vol.9, No.4, March 1983, pp. 393-402.
35. Leslie Isler, Edward T. Poppu and Scott Ward, "Children's Purchase Requests and Parental Responses Results from a Dairy Study", *Journal of Advertising Research*, Vol. 27, October/ November 1987, pp. 28-39.

36. Scott Ward and Daniel B. Wackman, "Children's Purchase Influence Attempts and Parental Yielding", *Journal of Marketing Research*, Vol. 9, No. 3, August 1972, pp. 316-319.

37. Ellen Foxman, Partriya Tansuhaj and Karen Ekstrom, "Adolescents Influence in Family Purchase Decisions; A Socialisation Perspective", *Journal of Business Research*, Vol.18 (Second Issue), 1989, pp. 159-172.

38. Lewis A. Berey and Richard W. Pollay, "The Influencing Role of the Child in Family Decision Making", *Journal of Marketing Research*, Vol.5, No.1, February, 1968, pp. 70-72.

39. George P. Moschis, "The Role of Family Communication in Consumer Socialisation of Children and Adolescents", *Journal of Consumer Research*, Vol. 11, No. 4, March 1985, pp. 898-913.

40. Les Carlson and Sanford Grossbart, "Parental Style and Consumer Socialisation of Children", *Journal of Consumer Research*, Vol.15, No.1, June 1988, pp. 77-94.

41. Raghbir Singh and Pavleen Kaur, "Do Rural and Urban Families Decide Differently to Buy?", *The ICFAI Journal of Marketing Management*, August 2004, pp.17-27.

Review of Literature

Introduction

Since the present study is related to family purchase decisions of durable goods, literature survey has been done regarding the theory and concepts of spousal purchase decision, process of family decision making and durable goods. During literature survey it is found that varieties of research problems have been explored in the concept and theory of spousal decision-making in western countries rather than in India.

Review of Literature

The findings of a few such research works have been presented below in chronological order.

Davis (1970)[1] has selected automobile and furniture to study the dimensions of husband and wife roles in consumer purchase decision and to analyse the extent of husband's and wife's agreements in their perception of roles. The relative influence of six automobile purchase decisions is positively associated and high. Data from husbands yield gammas and the degree of association reported by wives is even stronger. The same pattern characterises the association between relative influences in furniture purchase decisions. In contract to the association among decision roles within each of the two product categories, there is little relationship across product categories. There is an inverse relationship between influence in automobile purchase decision and influence in the purchase of furniture.

Fry and Siller (1970)[2] have designed a study to compare elements of the purchase decision processes of working and middleclass housewives, under the relatively controlled condition of a simulated shopping behaviour. Comparison of search, brand preference and deal sensitivity measures for the two social classes reveal a fairly high degree of similarity in observed behaviour during the shopping simulation. However differences found between the class groups in the sign and/or magnitude of variables relate to observed behaviour variation by social class in the nature of decision-making process which have been summarised in terms of subjective *vs.* objective relation sets.

Courtney and Lockeretz (1971)[3] has surveyed different magazines to study the role of women in magazine advertisement and it was found that the print advertisements rarely showed women in working roles. The distribution of occupational and non-working roles in the advertisements reinforces the feminists impression that women are rarely shown engaged in important activities outside the home and women are limited even in household decision making. They appear independently only for inexpensive purchases and for expensive purchases men are brought into the advertisements.

Davis (1971)[4] has proposed a multitrait-multi method approach for determining convergent and discriminant validity for the measurement of purchase influence. The four traits used in this study to measure purchase influence are global measure of influence, Blood and Wolfe index, seven role of purchase decisions for automobile and furniture. The findings show relatively high correlations between the Blood and Wolfe index and the seven automobile decisions for both husbands and wives.

Jeffrey (1971)[5] in his studies says that one of the key variables in studying the role of risk handling in the consumer decision process is self confidence. When making problem solving purchase choice decisions, low self confidence consumers would be defensive or indecisive and would tend to reject persuasive inputs.

Ward and Wackman (1972)[6] have examined the influence of demographics, parent-child interaction and mother's mass communication behaviour on children's purchase influence attempts and parental yielding. Analysis of marginal data indicates that children frequently attempt to influence purchases for food products but these attempts decrease with age. Durables which the children use directly are the second most requested product. Mothers of younger children (5-7 years old) indicate frequent influence attempts for game and toy purchases. While mothers of older children indicate frequent purchase influence attempts for clothing and record albums.

Another result of continuing study of consumer decision making directed by Newman and Staelin (1972)[7] has been made with an objective that knowledge of information seeking is fundamental to understand buyer behaviour and planning marketing communication and retail distribution. It is found that the amount of information seeking is positively related to decision time. The data also shows that experienced buyers are able to collect a lot amount of information in a short time. Young, unmarried persons have the highest information seeking scores as they have less experience. The study suggests that the purchase decision process for durables frequently begins with anticipation of product breakdown.

A study of activity in the purchase decision process and analysis of brand loyalty has been made by Newman and Werbel (1973)[8] by selecting six major appliances like refrigerator, washing machine, range, T.V. and air conditioner. To measure brand loyalty a scoring scheme has been adopted and it is found that 26.5 per cent of the households are brand loyal.

Davis and Rigauz (1974)[9] have examined the influence exerted by husbands and wives at different stages in the decision process for 25 economic decision in a convenience sample of Belgiam households in which both spouses are questioned. The analysis considers changes in marital rates throughout decision making and extent of role consensus within families by dividing the relative influence into four decision areas as 'husband dominant', 'wife dominant' or as a 'syncratic' or "autonomic" pattern.

Hempel (1974)[10] has measured the husband and wife interaction in family decision at different stages in the house buying decisions. Two areas are selected for the study in different periods namely Connecticut in 1968 and North West England in 1971. Role performance in the purchase decisions appeals to depend upon the type and nature of decisions – husbands are more involved in decisions concerning mortgage, price and when to buy while wives are more involved in decisions regarding neighbourhood and house style.

A study concerned with changes that have occurred over the past eighteen years in the roles of husband and wives in family purchase decision-making has been made by Cunningham and Green (1974).[11] The study made by Shart and Mott in 1955 and the study made by Robert in 1973 are compared. In the case of grocery, in 1955 the decision on how much to spend on groceries was dominated by wife and in 1973 the study found that this area was even more wife dominated. The comparative findings with respect to the decision of life insurance show that in 1955, 43 per cent of the decision was made by the husband and in 1973 it was 66 per cent. The automobile decision findings suggest a different tendency. The 1973 result shows more joint decision making than was in the case in 1955 study.

A study made by Hansen et al., (1975)[12] is concerned with the roles of husbands and wives in the decision to purchase a home. Husbands and wives tend to agree that the husband is dominant in the decision to rent or buy and in the price decision of home while the wife is dominant in the floor plan, style and size of home decisions.

Cox (1975)[13] uses two alternative operational definitions to indicate the degree of adjustment between a husband and a wife. Results show that relationship between marriage and the RCP definition is found to be significant at .001 levels for all five orders. The hypothesised relationship between stage in the family life cycle and the RCP definition is also examined by means of both Kruskal-Wallis test and Anova and the relationship is found to be significant.

Green and Cunningham (1975),[14] on the basis of inventory scores, divide the respondents into conservatives, moderates and liberals. Ten products are selected for the study. On five of the products and services, the purchase decision patterns of husbands and wives are same for the three subject groups. Decisions relating to groceries are wife dominated in the three groups while life insurance decisions are husband dominated in the three groups. Furniture, housing and family savings tend to be jointly made in all three groups.

Shuptrine and Samuelson (1976)[15] have made a study which is a partial replication of the study made by Davis (1970). The results indicate that the role response of a partner in major purchase decisions is product specific. The findings also indicate that the partner who is dominant for most prepurchase decision components also tends to make the real decision to purchase.

Davis (1976)[16] attempts to review and evaluate the area of decision-making within the households. His article includes the involvement of family members in economic decisions, the process by which family decisions are made and the consequences of different family structures and decision-making styles.

Burns and Granbois (1977)[17] are of the view that measures of involvement, empathy and recognised authority are taken for each sub decision to investigate the possible role in moderating the need for resolving discrepant preferences. The average husband is more highly involved than the average wife with respect to automobile size, automobile make, body, style, price range, type of transmission, type of radio, method of financing, type of brakes and place of purchase. Only exterior colour and seat upholstery have lowest husband involvement.

Scanzoni (1977)[18] suggests two important dimensions in the change of sex roles. First dimension is that younger women are coming toward to take up jobs in the same way as members of the dominant group (men) have always done. A second and concomitant dimension of sex role changes pertains to women's relationships with their husbands. Consequently decisions have to be made and issues have to be dealt with that are rarely grappled with earlier.

A research has been made by Westbrook et al., (1978)[19] to find out how satisfied or dissatisfied consumers are with their experience in arriving at purchase decisions of major household durables. Data are collected from recent buyers and prospective buyers. Over all, this study suggests that consumers find enjoyment and satisfaction in their buying experiences for durables considerably more often than they find difficulty and discontent.

Atkin (1978)[20] has observed patterns of interactions between parents and children in supermarket to determine the processes and effects of decision-making in the selection of breakfast cereals. Observers have viewed the behaviour of parents and children at the cereal shelves and recorded the sequence of action along with the characteristics of the participants. The findings show that 46 per cent of the children pose a cereal 'demand' and an additional 20 per cent offer a cereal 'request'. The rate of positive versus negative parental response is slightly higher in the demand than in the request situation. Most of the parent initiated sequences involve an invitation for the child to select a cereal. In majority of these cases, the child chooses a brand and the parent agrees to the selection.

Curry and Menasco (1979)[21] report some theoretical results based on one possible orientation for studying the husband-wife decision process. This orientation builds on research using the Weighted Linear Multiattribute (WLM) model of preference. The result demonstrates that marketing communication can often be effective without having to promote strong changes in weights. In the context of a joint decision, a message that attempts to increase each individual's weight for a particular attribute will not only improve the brand's utility but also increase agreement about this utility.

Filiatrault and Ritchie (1980)[22] have made a study concerning a series of 17 sub-decisions related to vocation travel and choice of accommodation during travel by comparing influence structure of two types of household DMU (family verses couple). The result shows that husbands tend to dominate decision-making more in family DMU than in those where no children are present and joint decision making is more prevalent in couple DMU's. Within family DMUs children have exerted little influence on the overall decision process.

Schaninger and Allen (1981)[23] have classified wife's occupational status as non-working wife (NWW), low-occupational status working wife (LSW) and high occupational status working wife (HSW) in order to present empirical support for a trichotomous family classification scheme of consumer behaviour. The results show that LSW wives purchased more number of dresses than NWW wives. Regarding ownership of T.V, LSW families tended to own more televisions especially, colour televisions more than HSW or NWW families. For the ownership of major and minor appliances such as microwaves, dishwashers, cloth washers, refrigerators, etc., both LSW and HSW families tend to own multi feature washers and dryers compared to NWW families. Higher mean feature counts for refrigerators and ranges are found for HSW families.

A study has been made by Reilly (1982)[24] to examine the use of convenience foods and the ownership of time saving durables for working wife and non-working wife families. It is found that it is negatively related to working and convenience food consumption. The model proposed by the author concludes that there is relationship between the wife's work status and the family's consumption behaviour. But there is lack of relationship among the wife's education, the family status and the wives work involvement.

Park (1982)[25] has examined the joint decision-making process using a method called the "decision plan net" in the context of a husband and wife's joint decision in home purchasing. Theoretical characterisations of joint decision making as a muddling-through process are discussed and a decision plan net is introduced for future decision situations. This study has conceptualised joint decision as a muddling-through process characterised by limited knowledge and awareness of each spouse's decision strategies.

Spiro (1983)[26] has examined the strategies used by individual spouses in making accommodative joint decisions for major durable purchases. People who are more traditional in their life styles and attitudes are more likely to use persuasive influence. This study identifies two major dimensions that affect influence choice. Several demographic and attitude variables such as traditional family ideology, avoidance of conflict, income, gender, age, age of youngest child, education, wife's employment and income of wife are the important discriminators among the influence strategies.

Krishnamurthi (1983)[27] is of the opinion that the use of key informants and assessment of relative influence may represent progress in understanding decision-making. The findings indicate that the views of others must be salient to the key informant and that a key informant must be knowledgeable of other's preferences if she/he is to represent the group's preferences accurately.

A study has been made by Weinberg and Winer (1983)[28] which is a duplicate of the study made by Strober and Weinberg in 1977 in which they have hypothesised that expenditure on durable goods is a function of total family income (Y), life cycle stage of family (Young), the family moving into a new home (MOVHSREC) and working women. The results show that wife's employment is not significantly related to the purchase of five time-saving durables such as dishwashers, dryers, refrigerators, stoves and washers.

A research study made by Slama and Armin (1985)[29] has developed a Likert-type scale to measure final consumer's involvement with the purchasing activity. By using ANOVA, it is found that members of the family life cycle with children have higher purchasing involvement than those without children at home. The ANOVA results also show a positive and direct relationship between education and purchasing involvement. Women have higher level of purchasing involvement but working wives' involvement in purchasing shows insignificant difference with traditional housewives.

Lehmann and Corfman (1987)[30] have developed a conceptual framework for conflict resolution and relative influence in cooperative groups and performed an exploratory test of these models on family making realistic consumption decisions as an initial indication of the framework's ability to represent group decisions. From the results of estimating these models it is concluded that relative preference intensity and decision history dominate the conflict resolution process.

Qualls (1987)[31] has made a study to examine the household decision behaviour and provide the theoretical justification for selecting the household dimensions which are then investigated in a sex role oriented theoretical model of household decision behaviour. The results show that Sex Role Orientation (SRO) is positively and significantly related to family member influence and mode of conflict resolution.

Ramu (1988)[32] has conducted a study in Bangalore city among 245 single-earner and double-earner couples. He has used the decision-making power of women as an indicator of her status in the family. The findings suggest that decision making power and economic resources is positively related. Thus wife's economic status enhances her importance in the domestic decision-making.

Bryant's (1988)[33] study on durables and wife's employment shows that wife's time and durables are complementary rather than substitutes and the effect of wife's employment on durable purchases is negative. As the wife's involvement in employment grows larger, the demand for durables falls. Durables are not substituted for the time wives spend on household activities as wives become more involved in the labour market.

Foxman et al., (1989)[34] have investigated the reports of the relationship among different members of the family regarding the adolescents' relative decision influence for specific products and of their general influence in family decision processes. Children tend to rate themselves as having more influence than their parents in purchasing toothpaste for themselves. Regarding clothes for the child, the respondents have indicated that children have a greater say in purchasing their own clothes. Higher the adolescents grades the less disagreement there is among family members regarding adolescent influence in family decision processes.

An article written by Menasco and Curry (1989)[35] has presented results from an experiment that addresses certain hypotheses about husband-wife choice behaviour in the context of the maximisation of dyadic utility. Results suggest that dyads tend to compromise, seeking balance and equity in outcomes. The forces that prompt equitable choices are grounded in principle, conflict avoidance and empathy.

A segmentation model in which demographic information is used to identify durable replaces segment is proposed in the study made by Bayus and Mehta (1995).[36] Data concerning the ownership of several home appliances including colour T.V., refrigerators, clothes washers, vacuum cleaners and coffee makers are collected. For colour T.V., more established households tend to be average replacers. Households with more adults tend to be early coffee maker replacers and average refrigerator replacers. Households with a high income tend to be early colour T.V. replacers and average coffee maker replacers. For vacuum cleaners households with children older than 6 years of age tend to be early replacers. Households with strong homemaking interests tend to be early replacers of refrigerators and none of the available household characteristics are statistically significant for cloth washers.

Kim and Lee (1997)[37] using reports from father, mother and child has developed family level measures of children's relative influence in family purchase decisions involving four categories of products that exhibit convergent and discriminant validity.

Palan and Robert (1997)[38] have explored the strategies used by adolescents to influence decision outcomes; the responses by parents to these influence attempts and the perceived effectiveness of these influence attempts. Bargaining, persuasion, emotional, legitimate and directive strategies are used by adolescents to influence parent decisions. Regarding the responses by parents, can't afford tactic, making delay, suggestion of alternative purchase choices on shopping location, reasoning and money deals are used to influence their attempts.

Arora and Allenby (1999)[39] have developed, tested and validated a statistical model that provides an outcome based or inferred measure of influence on family decision making involving a husband and a wife. They also have made an empirical analysis involving two family decisions making tasks (microoven and lawn mower) in which husbands and wives are expected to differ. The results show that for micro-oven on average wives have higher influences with regard to the burning power, cleaning pattern and price. For lawn mower on an average husbands have a substantially higher influence on all attributes.

Allen et al., (2001)[40] have compared individuals who are remarried with those in their first marriages investigating their standards for how marriages should be in the domains of autonomy and decision-making power and their reported communication patterns. It is found that marital communication is a major way in which spouses may change from a first marriage to a remarriage. Self reports in a remarriage indicate that they avoid discussing difficult issues and remarried spouses endorse standards for shared decision making power and more autonomy.

Jejeebhoy and Sathar (2001)[41] has compared the autonomy of women in three settings—Punjab in Pakistan and Uttar Pradesh and Tamil Nadu in India. The findings show that when women from all three sites are considered,

Tamil Muslims exhibit far greater level of autonomy than both Hindu and Muslim respondents from Uttar Pradesh and respondents from Punjab and concludes that in comparison, the influence of religion and nationality are less consistent and powerful.

Aribara et al., (2002)[42] have developed a hierarchical Bayes Model of group decision-making that incorporates preference revision and concession at the attribute level during the decision process. They find preference revision and concession to be strongly associated with sex, age and education. They have also found that converging preferences because of revision affect a member's concession which in turn affects post decision satisfaction.

Jejeebhoy (2002)[43] explores similarities and differences in the perceptions of rural Indian women and their husbands with regard to women's autonomy in terms of decision making, physical mobility and access to resources in Uttar Pradesh and Tamil Nadu. The results show that women from Tamil Nadu, regardless of religion, have significantly more decision making authority and mobility than women in Uttar Pradesh and have considerably greater access to economic resources.

Nash' bargaining approach to household behaviour has been tested by Lakshmanasamy (2002-03)[44] who studied the effect of pooled non labour income *vs.* independent labour incomes of both the husband and wife on five household decisions *viz.,* male and female labour supply, household expenditure on food, education and health. The empirical testing of unitary *vs.* collective models of this study shows that, in the Indian household context, female independent non-labour income is insignificant and it may not have any significant influence on female's bargaining strength and her control over household resource allocation decisions. Hence the collective models to household behaviour have limited scope in the context of the Indian household behaviour.

Shivakumar and Ravindran (2003)[45] in their study on "The Role of Husband and Wife in Purchase Decisions" in Pondicherry region have found out that it is the wife who takes the decision regarding the purchase of agarbattis, cooking oil, grocery, milk and salt. The husband is the decision maker for fruits and magazines. Mosquito mats/ coils are bought on the basis of joint decisions. It is found that there is significant difference in the decision regarding the purchase of convenience goods due to changes in the personal characteristics of husband.

Su Chenting et al., (2003)[46] are of the opinion that spousal decision behaviour is the key to understanding how families reach purchase decisions. Spousal decision behaviour is affected by prior decision experiences and this forms the basis of future interactions. The results indicate that: (*i*) both husband and wife tend not to reciprocate coercion in a discrete purchase decision; (*ii*) both husband and wife tend not to use strong means of influence across decisions consistently; and (*iii*) both husband and wife's post decision evaluations tend to affect subsequent decision behaviour.

Grewal et al., (2004)[47] in their study "The Timing of Repeat Purchases of Consumer Durable Goods" show that actual purchase decisions and hazard models that incorporate individual heterogeneity, support the suggested role of attitude functions in explaining and predicting interpurchase intervals and suggest means by which managers can position their products to shorten interpurchase intervals. Communication and positioning strategies that help consumers achieve social goals and fit into desired social settings would help firms increase the rate of repurchase of consumer durables.

Raghbir Singh and Pavleen Kaur (2004)[48] in their study on role structure for product purchase decision across urban and rural families brings forth that husbands in urban families wield maximum influence for purchase of two-wheeler whereas wives have greater influence in the purchase of a refrigerator. Both spouses together have the strongest influence on all durables. Children exercise little influence over durable purchase while all the members together use the greatest power for purchase of television and two-wheeler. In the rural, more control is wielded by both husband and wife for the purchase of all durables except that of car, which is influenced by all the members of the family. For automobile husbands alone or jointly they decide about the time of purchase. Store selection decision is dominated by husband. Regarding budget decision role in the urban, husbands demonstrate considerable power.

Viswanathan (2005)[49] and others have made a study of how functionally illiterate consumers behave and make decisions while shopping. It reveals cognitive predilections, trade offs and coping behaviours that distinguish functionally illiterate consumers from literate consumers. The authors find that functionally illiterate consumers display distinct cognitive predilections such as concrete reasoning and pictographic thinking when making sense of elements of the marketing mix such as packaging, in-store displays and price promotions.

A study on brand consciousness among children and its effect on family buying behaviour have been made by Nithila (2006)[50] in Bangalore city. Data is collected both from children and parents through two set of questionnaire. Regarding brand awareness among children there is a very high degree of brand awareness among children. But the children declare that they do not enjoy independence in decision-making for the items listed. According to parents view for items such as chocolates, chips and soft drinks the children are allowed to decide independently and not for the durable goods like watches, clothes, bags as they are relatively more expensive.

Mohanram and Mahavi (2007)[51] attempt to evaluate the factors influencing teenagers in forming purchase decision for two-wheelers in Chennai (TN, India). Teenagers are influenced by updated information of the product like price, technology and peer compulsion and sales talk of the dealers.

They employ two types of strategies to convince their parents—emotional and logical. They give top priority to quality, durability, utility and long term benefits. They also look at colour, popularity, physical appearance and brand value. However for promotional mix, they are driven by dealers' sales initiative, cultural environment stimuli, sales promotion and advertisement. The emotional teenagers give least importance to sales promotion like offers and schemes whereas teenagers who approach logically consider offer and schemes as important.

Conclusion

The study on family decision making has attracted many researchers throughout the world and recently it has got some attraction in India. It is evident from the review presented that attempts are being made to study the process of family decision making. However, reviews reveal that not much effort has been made in India to analyse the 'women' factor in family purchase decision of durable goods. The present study is therefore, focused to fill the gap with this regard.

REFERENCES

1. Harry L. Davis, "Dimensions of Marital Roles in Consumer Decision Making", *Journal of Marketing Research*, Vol.VII, No.2, May 1970, pp.168-77.
2. Joseph N. Fry and Fredrick H. Siller, "A Comparison of Housewife Decision Making in Two Social Classes", *Journal of Marketing Research*, Vol.VII, No.3, August 1970, pp.333-37.
3. Alice E. Courtney and Sarah Wernick Lockeretz, "A Woman's Place: An Analysis of the Roles Portrayed by Women in Magazine Advertisements", *Journal of Marketing Research*, Vol.8, No.1, February 1971, pp.92-95.
4. Harry L. Davis, "Measurement of Husband-Wife Influence in Consumer Purchase Decisions", *Journal of Marketing Research*, Vol.VIII, No.3, August 1971, pp.305-12.
5. Jeffrey, A. Barach, "Consumer Decision Making and Self Confidence", *Indian Journal of Marketing*, Vol.2, No.3, September 1971, p.18.

6. Scott Ward and Daniel B. Wackman, "Children's Purchase Influence Attempts and Parental Yielding", *Journal of Marketing Research*, Vol.IX, No.3, August 1972, pp.316-319.
7. Joseph W. Newman and Richard Staelin, "Pre Purchase Information Seeking for New Cars and Major Household Appliances", *Journal of Marketing Research*, Vol.IX, No.3, August 1972, pp.249-57.
8. Joseph W. Newman and Richard A. Werbel, "Multivariate Analysis of Brand Loyalty for Major Household Appliances", *Journal of Marketing Research*, Vol.X, No.4, November 1973, pp.404-409.
9. Harry L. Davis and Benny P. Rigaux, "Perception of Marital Roles in Decision Processes", *Journal of Consumer Research*, Vol.1, No.1, June 1974, pp.51-62.
10. Donald J. Hempel, "Family Buying Decisions: A Cross Cultural Perspective", *Journal of Marketing Research*, Vol.XI, No.3, August 1974, pp.295-302.
11. Isabella C.N. Cunningham and Robert T. Green, "Purchasing Roles in the U.S. Family 1955 and 1973", *Journal of Marketing*, Vol.38, No.4, October 1974, pp.61-81.
12. Gary M. Munsinger, Jean E. Weber and Richard W. Hansen, "Joint Home Purchasing Decisions by Husbands and Wives", *Journal of Consumer Research*, Vol.1, No.4, March 1975, pp.60-66.
13. Eli P. Cox, "Family Purchase Decision Making and the Process of Adjustment", *Journal of Marketing Research*, Vol.XII, No.2, May 1975, pp.189-95.
14. Robert T. Green and Isabella Cunningham, C.M., "Feminine Role Perception and Family Purchasing Decision", *Journal of Marketing Research*, Vol.XII, No.3, August 1975, pp.325-32.
15. Shuptrine, F.K., and Samuelson, G., "Dimensions of Marital Roles in Consumer Decision Making: Revisited", *Journal of Marketing Research*, Vol.XIII, No.1, February 1976, pp.87-91.
16. Harry L. Davis, "Decision Making Within the Household ", *Journal of Consumer Research*, Vol.2, No.4, March 1976, pp.241-260.
17. Alvin C. Burns and Donald H. Granbois, "Factors Moderating the Resolutions of Preference Conflict in Family Automobile Purchasing", *Journal of Marketing Research*, Vol.XIV, No.1, February 1977, pp.77-86.
18. John Scanzoni, "Changing Sex Roles and Emerging Directions in Family Decision Making", *Journal of Consumer Research*, Vol.4, No.3, December 1977, pp.185-88.

19. Robert A. Westbrook, Joseph Newman and James R. Taylor, "Satisfaction/ Dissatisfaction in the Purchase Decision Process", *Journal of Marketing*, Vol.43, No.4, October 1978, pp.54-60.

20. Charles K. Atkin, "Observation of Parent Child Interaction in Supermarket Decision Making", *Journal of Marketing*, Vol.42, No.4, October 1978, pp.41-45.

21. David J. Curry and Michael B. Menasco, "Some Effects of Differing Information Processing Strategies on Husband-Wife Joint Decisions", *Journal of Consumer Research*, Vol.6, No.2, September 1979, pp.192-203.

22. Pierre Filiatrault and Brent Ritchie, J.R., "Joint Purchasing Decisions: A Comparison of Influence Structure in Family and Couple Decision Making Units", *Journal of Consumer Research*, Vol.7, No.2, September 1980, pp.131-140.

23. Charles M. Schaninger and Chris T. Allen, "Wife's Occupational Status as a Consumer Behaviour Construct", *Journal of Consumer Research*, Vol.8, No.2, September 81, pp.189-196.

24. Michael D. Reilly, "Working Wives and Convenience Consumption", *Journal of Consumer Research*, Vol.8, No.4, March 1982, pp.407-418.

25. Whan Park, C., "Joint Decisions in Home Purchasing: A Muddling-Through Process", *Journal of Consumer Research*, Vol.9, No.2, September 1982, pp.151-162.

26. Rosann L. Spiro, "Persuasion in Family Decision-Making", *Journal of Consumer Research*, Vol.9, No.4, March 1983, pp.393-402.

27. Lakshman Krishnamurthi, "The Salience of Relevant Others and its Effect on Individual and Joint Preference: An Experimental Investigation", *Journal of Consumer Research*, Vol.10, No.1, June 1983, pp.62-72.

28. Charles B. Weinberg and Russell S. Winer, "Working Wives and Major Family Expenditures: Replication and Extension", *Journal of Consumer Research*, Vol.10, No.2, September 1983, pp.259-263.

29. Mark E. Slama and Armen Tashchian, "Selected Socio-economic and Demographic Characteristics Associated with Purchasing Involvement", *Journal of Marketing*, Vol.49, No.1, Winter 1985, pp.72-82.

30. Kim P. Corfman and Donald R. Lehmann, "Models of Co-operative Group Decision Making and Relative Influence: An Experimental Investigation of Family Purchase Decision", *Journal of Consumer Research*, Vol.14, No.1, June 1987, pp.1-13.

31. William J. Qualls, "Household Decision Behaviour: The Impact of Husbands' and Wives' Sex Role Orientation", *Journal of Consumer Research*, Vol.14, No.4, September 1987, pp.264-279.
32. Ramu, G.N., "Wife's Economic Status and Marital Power: A Case of Single and Dual Earner Couples", *Sociological Bulletin*, Vol.37 (182), March-September 1988, pp.49-69.
33. Keith Bryant, W., "Durables and Wives' Employment Yet Again" *Journal of Consumer Research*, Vol.15, No.1, June 1988, pp.37-47.
34. Ellen R. Foxman, Patriya S. Tansuhaj and Karin M. Ekstrom, "Family Member's Perceptions of Adolescents' Influence in Family Decision Making', *Journal of Consumer Research*, Vol.15, No.4, March 1989, pp.482-491.
35. Michael B. Menasco and David J. Curry, "Utility and Choice: An Empirical Study of Wife/Husband Decision Making", *Journal of Consumer Research*, Vol.16, No.1, June 1989, pp.87-97.
36. Barry L. Bayus and Raj Mehta, "A Segmentation Model for the Targeted Marketing of Consumer Durables", *Journal of Marketing Research*, Vol.XXXII, No.4, November 1995, pp.463-468.
37. Chankon Kim and Hanjoon Lee, "Development of Family Triadic Measures for Children's Purchase Influence", *Journal of Marketing Research*, Vol.XXXIV, No.3, August 1997, pp. 307-321.
38. Kay M. Palan and Robert E. Wilkes, "Adolescent-Parent Interaction in Family Decision Making", *Journal of Consumer Research*, Vol.24, No.2, September 1997, pp. 159-169.
39. Neeraj Arora and Greg M. Allenby, "Measuring the Influence of Individual Preference Structures in Group Decision Making", *Journal of Marketing Research*, Vol.XXXVI, No.4, November 1999, pp.476-487.
40. Elizabeth Sandin Allen, Donald H. Baucom, Chares K. Burnett, Norman Epstein and Lyn A. Rankin Esquer, "Decision-Making Power, Autonomy and Communication in Remarried Spouses Compared with First-Married Spouses", *Family Relations*, Vol. 50, No. 4, 2001, pp. 326-334.
41. Shireen T. Jejeebhoy and Zeba A. Sathar, "Women's Autonomy in India and Pakistan: The Influence of Religion and Region", *Population and Development Review*, Vol. 27, No. 4, December 2001, pp. 687-712.
42. Anocha Aribara, Neeraj Arora and Onur Bodur, "Understanding the Role of Preference Revision and Concession in Group Decisions", *Journal of Marketing Research*, Vol. XXXIX, No. 3, August 2002, pp. 336-349.

43. Shireen T. Jejeebhoy, "Convergence and Divergence in Spouses Perspectives on Women's Autonomy in Rural India", *Studies in Family Planning*, Vol. 33, No. 4, December 2002, pp. 299-308.
44. Lakshmanasamy, L., "Nash Bargained Household Decisions; Testing the Economic Models of Family in India", *Indian Economic Journal*, Vol. 50, Nos. 3 & 4, 2002-03, pp. 99-108.
45. Shivakumar, K., and Ravindran, R., "Role of Husband and Wife in Purchase Decisions", *Facts For You*, Vol.23, No.8, May 2003, pp. 29-31.
46. Chenting Su., Edward F. Fern and Keying Ye, "A Temporal Dynamic Model of Spousal Family Purchase-Decision Behaviour", *Journal of Marketing Research*, Vol.XL, No.3, August 2003, pp. 268-281.
47. Grewal Rajdeep, Raj Mehta and Frank R. Kardes, "The Timing of Repeat Purchases of Consumer Durable Goods; The Role of Functional Bases of Consumer Attitudes", *Journal of Marketing Research*, Vol.XLI, No.1, February 2004, pp. 45-61.
48. Raghbir Singh and Pavleen Kaur, "Do Rural and Urban Families Decide Differently to Buy?", *The ICFAI Journal of Marketing Management*, August 2004, pp. 17-27.
49. Viswanathan Madhubalan et al., "Decision Making and Coping of Functionally Illiterate Consumers and Some Implications for Marketing Management", *Journal of Marketing*, Vol.69, No.1, January 2005, pp. 15-31.
50. Nithila Vincent, "A Study on Brand Consciousness among Children and Its Effect on Family Buying Behaviour in Bangalore City", *Indian Journal of Marketing*, Vol.XXXVI, No.1, January 2006, pp. 12-18.
51. Mohanram, A.S., and Mahavi, C., "Product related Characteristics, Promotion and Marketing Mix are Key Tools in Determining Purchase Behaviour and Purchase Decision by Teenagers—An Empirical Study", *Indian Journal of Marketing*, Vol. XXXVII, No. 2, February 2007, pp. 3-12.

Consumer Decision Making

Introduction

Consumer decision making is the process by which consumers make purchasing decisions. Consumer decision-making is not a single process. It depends upon the type of decision making and the involvement of consumers in the purchase. The process of decision-making describes the processes which consumers go through before, during and after making a purchase.

This chapter deals with the consumers decision making process.

Consumer Decision Making Process

The process of consumer decision making has five steps. It begins with a problem or a need recognition that the consumers have a problem that can be solved by making a purchase. Depending on how important the purchase is they engage in some kind of information search—which is as simple as scanning our memories for a reminder of what product is bought in the past to solve a similar problem or as extensive as a complete review of a product information or a mall to mall shopping expedition. Once they feel they have enough information to make a good decision, alternative evaluation begins to compare different solutions, their cost and benefits. In a number of instances information search and alternative evaluation occur at the same time. Finally they make a choice to buy a specific product with specific features from a specific outlet and at a specific price that provides the benefits they are looking for.

The following chart illustrates the various types of consumer decision processes. As the consumer moves from a very low level of involvement with the purchase to a high level of involvement, decision making becomes increasingly complex.

Chart 3.1. Involvement and Types of Decision Making[1]

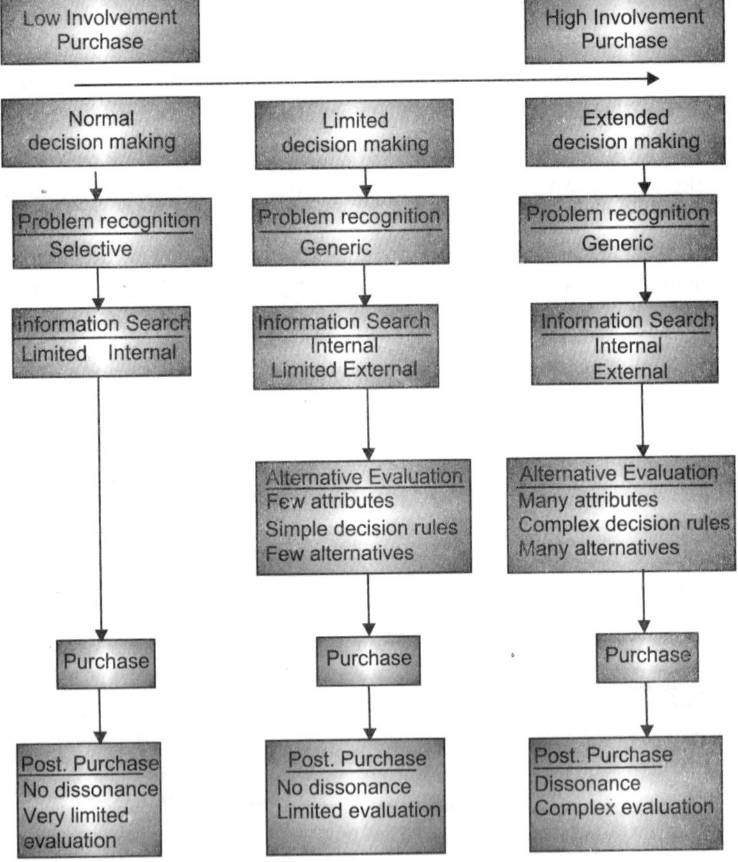

Purchase Involvement

Purchase involvement is defined as the level of concern for, or interest in, the purchase process triggered by the need to consider a particular purchase.[2]

Purchase involvement is a temporary state of an individual or household. It is influenced by the interaction of individual, product, and situational characteristics.[3]

It is an internal state that the consumer experiences before purchasing a product. High involved consumer is one who is very interested in finding out the differences among different brands of a product and is willing to invest considerable energy in decision-making about purchasing them.

Low involved consumers are passive receivers of information who engage in virtually no active information search about alternative brands. Advertisements or other information will be processed at a very superficial level receiving little meaningful evaluation. Very low levels of brand awareness and comprehension will be the result.

Kinds of Decision Making

Normal Decision Making

It involves no decision as it is a habitual decision making. In this kind a problem is recognised. Internal search provides a single preferred solution for brand. That brand is purchased and an evaluation occurs only if the brand fails to perform as expected. Normal decisions occur when there is very low involvement with the purchase. At the shop, the normal decision maker picks up the product without considering alternative brands, its price or other potentially relevant factors.

Limited Decision Making

It involves internal and limited external search, few alternatives, simple decision rules on a few attributes and little post-purchase evaluation. It covers the middle ground between nominal decision making and extended decision making.

Limited decision making also occurs in response to some emotional or environmental needs. If the consumers are bored with the current product then they may purchase a new brand. This decision might involve evaluating only the newness or novelty of the available alternatives or evaluate a purchase in terms of the actual or anticipated behaviour of others.

Extended Decision Making

This involves an extensive internal and external information search followed by a complex evaluation of multiple alternatives and significant post purchase evaluation. It is the response to a high level of purchase involvement. After the purchase, doubt about its correctness is likely and a thorough evaluation of the purchase takes place.

Purchase of Durable Goods and Decision Making

Deciding to purchase durable goods is rather an important and complex decision. In complex decision making, consumers evaluate brands in a detailed and comprehensive manner. More information is sought and more brands are evaluated than in other types of buying decision. Complex decision making is most likely when consumers are involved with the product. The complex decision making is most likely for

- High priced product
- Products associated with performance risks
- Complex products
- Products associated with one's ego.

The other facilitating conditions also exist. The most important is adequate time for extensive information search and processing. If decision must be made quickly complex decision making will not occur. A study by Greenleaf and Lehmann found that consumers sometimes delay a decision because of insufficient or inaccurate information.[4]

The Nature of Problem Recognition

Problem recognition is the first stage in the consumer decision process. Problem recognition is the result of a discrepancy between a desired state and an actual state that is sufficient to arouse and activate the desired process.[5] An actual state is the way an individual perceives his or her feelings and situations to be at the present time. A desired state is the way an individual wants to feel or be at the present time.

The kind of action taken by consumers in response to recognised problems relates directly to its importance to the consumer, the situation and the dissatisfaction or inconvenience created by the problem. Without recognition of a problem there is no need for a decision. When there is a discrepancy between a consumer desire and the perceived actual state, recognition of a problem occurs.

Process of Problem Recognition

Chart 3.2. Process of Problem Recognition[6]

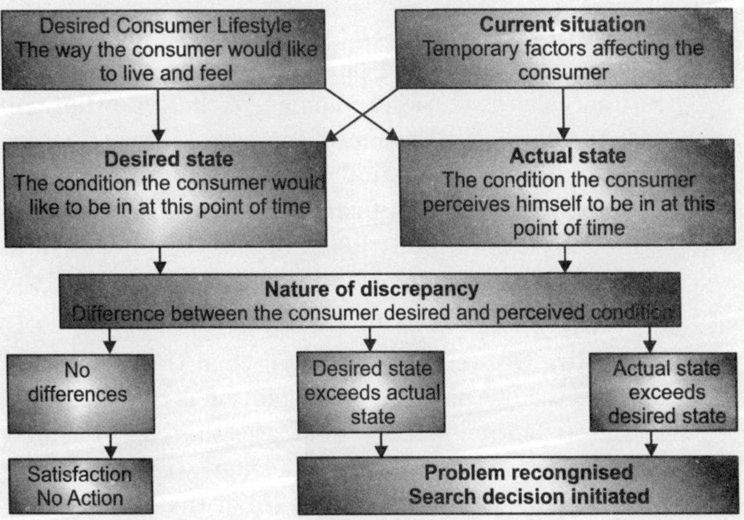

Types of Problems Recognition

Immediacy of problem solution is a relevant factor in determining the decision time horizon.[7] Importance of problem will be a significant factor influencing decisions within each category of problem recognition.

(*i*) **Routine Problems:** These are those in which the difference between actual and desired states is expected to occur and an immediate solution is required. Usually convenience goods are associated with this type of problem recognition. Both routine and emergency problems lead to what is known as 'at need' purchases of goods and services. These are having a minimal time lag between purchase and actual consumption.

(*ii*) **Emergency Problems:** These are those that are unexpected in which immediate solution is required. If the individual has little time to engage in shopping and in emergency situation, this problem is recognised. Some retailers cater to customers facing emergency problems.

(*iii*) **Planning Problems:** It occurs when the problem occurrence is expected but an immediate solution is not necessary. These problems are the type that can lead to purchase of 'pre-need' goods and services, which are bought in anticipation of being used in the future, generally after a significant time lag. The ability to put off a purchase may lead to more complicated and difficult purchasing problems later on or even the inability to purchase at all.

(*iv*) **Evolving Solutions:** It occurs when the problem is unexpected but no immediate solution is required. The fashion-adoption process illustrates this case. Fashion adoption ordinarily occurs over a lengthy period of time. Although one may become aware of the new fashion item's existence, there may be no initial desire to own that item. Over time, as the innovation spreads and more consumes buy the item, a discrepancy between the consumer's desired and actual state may develop and increase. The diffusion of an innovation involves the situation of evolving problems.

Result of Problem Recognition

Once the consumer becomes aware of a problem two basic outcomes are possible.

One result is for the consumer not to pursue any further problem solving behaviour which might occur if the difference between the consumer's perceived desire and actual state are not great enough to cause him to act to resolve the difference.

The second type of response that may occur from the problem recognition process is for the consumer to proceed into further stages of decision making activity by engaging in information search and evaluation.

Information Search

Once consumers have recognised the existence of a problem and assuming there are not constraints preventing further behaviour, they move on to the next stage in the decision making process. Producers and retailers must understand how consumers search for and evaluate information on possible purchase otherwise the information provided by them may be inappropriate and ineffective.

Types of Information Search

(*i*) **Pre Purchase Search:** This is the typical form of search associated within the purchasing context. If the consumer has recognized a problem, then pre purchase search would be engaged in.

(*ii*) **Ongoing Search:** This is characterised as search activities independent of specific needs or decisions. It does not occur in order to solve a recognised and immediate purchase problem. If a consumer is searching with an interest in a product but with no demand for the product, then the search would be an ongoing search.

(*iii*) **Internal Search:** This is the first stage that occurs after the consumer experiences problem recognition. It is a mental process of recalling and reviewing information stored in the memory that may relate to the purchase situation.[8] The consumer relies on any attitudes, information or past experiences that have been stored in memory and can be recalled for application to the problem at hand. The recall may be immediate or may occur slowly, as a conscious effort is made to bring the information to mind. Once recalled, the information may be used in the evaluation process as the consumer seeks to resolve the purchase decision.

(*iv*) **External Search:** This refers to the process of obtaining information from other sources in addition to that which can be recalled from memory. Some sources from which such information might be obtained are advertisements, friends, sales people, store displays and product related magazine. A study made by Newman[9] is of the opinion that many buyers are engaged in little information seeking.

Information Search on the Internet

More than half of the population now uses the Internet and more than a third of all consumers report using it for product or service information search.[10] So Internet is a preferred source of product-related information among Internet users. Thus Internet has become an important source of information for purchase decisions. Internet contains market supplied data in the form of advertisements associated with search, entertainment and general information sites and home pages or Internet presence sites.

The presence of website addresses in an advertisement enhances various aspects of the firm's image; customers also encounter ads on the Internet while visiting general information, search and entertainment sites. These are generally banner ads that when clicked will take the consumer to the company or product's home page.

Alternative Evaluation and Selection

Evaluation involves those activities undertaken by the consumer to appraise carefully, on the basis of certain criteria, alternative solutions to market related problems. The search process determines what the alternatives are, and in the evaluation process, they are compared so that the consumer is ready to make a decision.

Evaluative Criteria

A consumer evaluates a brand on the basis of a number of choice criteria. These criteria are the standards and specifications the consumer uses in evaluating products and brands.

Evaluative criteria may vary from one consumer to another. No matter how many criteria are evaluated by the consumer, they are likely to differ in their importance usually with one or two criteria being more important than others. So while several evaluative criteria are salient to the consumer, some are determinant. The marketer should be careful in assuming the features which are ranked as most important by consumers.

The number and type of evaluative criteria may vary by product. Consumers generally use few alternative criteria when purchasing grocery items but while purchasing durable goods more evaluative criteria would be used in the evaluation process. Similarly, consumers may use more criteria for high involvement products than for low-involvement ones.

Evaluative criteria may also change over time. As consumers gain new experiences and information this evaluative criteria may shift. When innovation appears with previously unknown features, consumers may begin to incorporate these features into their evaluative criteria. As they learn from marketers or friends there may be changes in their evaluative criteria.

Reducing the Range of Alternatives

During search the brand alternatives to the buyer's product choice decision are identified. Although there may be many brands in existence the consumer is not likely to be aware of all of them. Some brands will not be considered by the consumer because of unawareness. Brand names can be very valuable assets to a company. The marketer seeks to make consumers aware of the availability of his brand and to supply them with sufficient information to evaluate it and then to purchase.

There exists three subsets of brands within the awareness set of alternatives.

(*i*) **Evoked Set:** This set consists of the few selected brands evaluated positively by the consumer for purchase and consumption. These are the brands the consumer would be willing to consider further.

(*ii*) **Inert Set:** This set consists of those brands that the consumer has failed to perceive any advantage in buying as they are evaluated neither positively or negatively because the consumer may have insufficient information to evaluate.

(*iii*) **Inept Set:** This set is made up of brands that have been rejected from purchase consideration by the consumer because of an unpleasant experience or negative feedback. The brands in this set are evaluated negatively by the consumer and will not be considered at all in their present form.

Evaluating Alternatives

There are two approaches to know how consumers process the information gathered during the search process on their evoked set of brand. They are brand processing or attribute processing.

In brand processing the buyer assesses one brand at a time. The consumer may decide to look at a particular brand, examine several attributes of that brand and then assess several attributes for a second and third brand.

In attribute processing the consumer examines a specific attribute and then compares several other brands on that attribute. Then a second attribute may be selected for comparison.

Consumers may either use compensatory processes or non- compensatory processes as decision rule in evaluating product alternative attributes.

Non-Compensatory Decision Rules: Decision rules are said to be non compensatory when good performance on one evaluative criterion does not offset or compensate for poor performance on another evaluative criterion of the brand.

The following are the types of non compensatory decision-rules:

(*i*) **Disjunctive Rule:** This approach is used when the consumer establishes minimum acceptable performance standards which each brand must meet. Any brand will be acceptable if it exceeds the minimum standard of any criterion. The decision rule will then be to select the brand that exceeds the other by the greatest amount of the criterion selected.

(*ii*) **Conjunctive Rule:** This rule requires the consumer to establish minimum levels of acceptability on each brand attribute. For each evaluative criterion of importance to the consumer, a cut off point will be set below which brands would not be considered further.

(*iii*) **Lexicographic Rule:** This extension of the disjunctive decision rule allows additional evaluative criteria to be incorporated in the decision, if necessary. If a choice cannot be made by evaluating the most important criterion, other evaluative criteria will be assessed in their order of importance.

(*iv*) **Sequential Elimination Rule:** In this decision approach, the consumer has established acceptable performance minimum for each evaluative criterion and then proceeds to evaluate each brand and eliminate any which do not measure up to these minimums.

Compensatory Decision Rule: Consumers using a compensatory decision rule will allow perceived favourable ratings or brand evaluative criteria to offset unfavourable evaluations. Brand strengths can compensate for brand weaknesses. This approach uses more than one evaluative criterion for assessment by consumers. This decision rule evaluates brands individually along all dimensions or attributes with the overall evaluation being the sum of the weighted ratings along each attribute. The brand obtaining the highest sum would be the brand purchased by the consumer.

Purchase

By categorising purchases into those that are planned and those that are unplanned, marketers are better able to guide consumers through or encourage them to skip completely the alternative evaluation stage in decision making.

Types of Purchase Situations

There are four types of purchase situations.

(*i*) **A Specifically Planned Purchase:** A purchase in which the item and even the brand is decided before the consumer visits a store or investigates other outlet options.

(*ii*) **Generally Planned Purchase:** It is one in which a decision is made before visiting a store rather than an item from a certain product category will be purchased. The specific item and the brand are not yet decided. A purchase is also considered generally planned if the consumer has, even without considering product purchase as a solution, given thought to solving a problem.

(*iii*) **Substitute Purchase:** It is made when a consumer switches from a specifically or generally planned item to an altogether different one to purchase.

(*iv*) **Unplanned Purchase:** It is one that is made with no conscious prior consideration or need recognition. It is this type of purchase that is more likely than others to be triggered by some stimulus in the market place.

Outlet Selection

Gone are the days when a single marketer or a single marketing channel enjoyed exclusive distribution of unique products. Today, the moment a new product hits the market, dozens of imitators or parity products rapidly follow. They are not only available from retail stores but they are found on the web also.

There are an ever increasing array of outlets or distribution channels. Outside the homes, the consumer can visit retail stores, strip malls, discount malls, huge indoor shopping centers, or the new town centers. They can look at non-store locations such as flea markets, swap meets, auctions or even garage sales. Within the home they can shop from catalogs, fax machine, over the telephone, by watching television shopping channels or through a variety of sites on the Internet. The Internet has shaken up the retail options picture.

Outlet Image

Outlet image whether of a retail store, a catalog, a home shopping network or even a flea market has a great deal with why consumers choose to shop there. If there is a good match between the image of an outlet and the consumers own self-image, they are more likely to shop there. Outlet image results from a mix of functional and psychological attributes. Functional attributes include product selection, price ranges, credit policies, store layout and comparing competitions.

Image is very much in the eye of the beholder—it is what the consumer perceives it to be and it varies from person to person.[11]

Store Loyalty

Store loyalty refers to the consumer's inclination to patronise a given store during a specific period of time. Store loyalty can be a very important factor influencing the company's profits. Loyal customers will tend to concentrate their purchases on the store and may represent a very profitable market segment if they are identified. The store loyal's profile is one of a relatively conservative, inactive, time conscious, home town oriented person.

Paying for the Purchase

Cash and personal cheques are the most widely used methods of payment regardless of the type or cost of item or the place of business. For expensive durables, a major decision involves the nature of payment to be used in the purchase. Credit is another basis which attracts the consumers. Retailers adopt numerous ways to ease the payment decision. Making store check-outs easier facilitates the consumer's payment process. The use of electronic scanners at the point of check-out combined with compatible credit cards also makes the payment decision process easier and quicker.

Banks have also joined the move to facilitate purchase payment decisions. Not only numerous bank cards and loan plans are available but even after regular banking hours, electronic fund transfers may be made in order to obtain the necessary credit or cash with which to pay the purchases.

Post Purchase Consumer Behaviour

Knowing what happens after a sale is as important as understanding what causes consumers to buy. This is an understanding of actual rather than potential customers and purchase situations. Knowing both positive and negative post purchase behaviour is a very effective means through which goods and services can be improved, promotions better targeted and strategies reshaped both to keep current customers and to attract new ones.

The following figure illustrates the relationship among the post purchase processes.

Chart 3.3. Relationships among the Post Purchase Processes

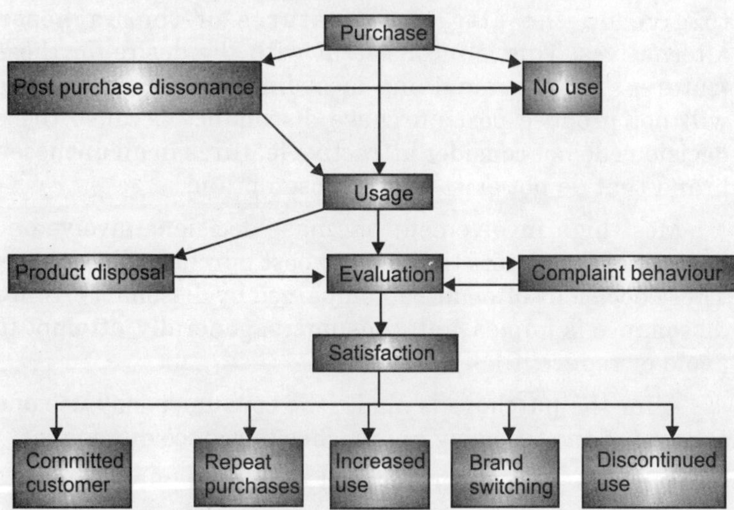

Post Purchase Dissonance

Consumers may become dissonant over a purchase decision. Cognitive dissonance emerges as a result of discrepancy between a consumer's decision and the consumer's prior evaluation. The probability and magnitude of dissonance may be because of:

- The degree of commitment of the decision. The easier it is to alter the decision, the less likely the consumer is to experience dissonance.
- The importance of the decision to the consumer. The more important the decision the more likely the dissonance will result.
- The difficulty of choosing among the alternatives. The more difficult it is to select from among the alternatives the more likely the experience and magnitude of dissonance will be.
- The individual's tendency to experience anxiety. The higher the tendency to experience anxiety, the more likely the individual will experience post purchase dissonance.

Dissonance occurs because making a relatively permanent commitment to a chosen alternative requires one to give up the attractive features of the unchosen alternatives. This is inconsistent with the desire for those features. Thus nominal and most limited decision-making will not produce post purchase dissonance because these decisions do not consider attractive features in an unchosen brand that do not exist in the chosen brand.

Most high involvement purchase decisions involve one or more of the factors that lead to post purchase dissonance. These decisions often are accompanied by dissonance. Since dissonance is unpleasant, consumers, generally, attempt to avoid or reduce it.

After the purchase is made, the consumer may use one or more of the following approaches to reduce dissonance.

- Increase the desirability of the brand purchased
- Decrease the desirability of rejected alternatives
- Decrease the importance of the purchase decision
- Reverse the purchase decision by returning the product before use.

But studies show that consumers find enjoyment and satisfaction in their buying experiences for durables considerably more often than they find difficulty and discontent.[12]

Product Disposition

Disposition of the product or the products container may occur before, during or after product use or the products can be completely consumed where no disposition may be involved. Product consumption does not end with purchase and use. The physical product, packaging and the promotional materials associated with it must be disposed of. Product disposition is the process of reselling, recycling, trashing, repairing, trading and the like associated with the physical product, packaging and its promotional materials, when no longer perceived as useful by the consumer or marketer.

This has become an increasingly important issue in the world of growing population size, limited space, limited national resources and high levels of manufacture. So disposition is considered as a critical part of consumption behaviour.

Post Purchase Evaluation

The consumer is uncertain of the wisdom of his decision. He rethinks the decision in the post purchase stage. Rethinking broadens the consumer's set of experiences stored in memory. It provides a check on how well he is doing as a consumer in selecting products and stores. The feedback that the consumer receives from this stage helps to make adjustments in future purchasing strategies. For many products, this is a dynamic process, with the factors that drive satisfaction evolving overtime.[13]

While and after using the product, service or outlet, the consumer will perceive some level of performance. This perceived performance level could be noticeably above the expected level, noticeably below the expected level or at the expected level.

A brand, whose perceived performance fails to confirm expectations, generally produces dissatisfaction. If the discrepancy between performance and expectation is large, the consumer may restart the entire decision process. When perceptions of product performance match expectations that are at or above the minimum desired performance levels, satisfaction generally results. Satisfaction reduces the level of decision-making, the next time.[14]

Dissatisfaction Responses

A product, the perceived performance of which fails to confirm expectations, generally produces dissatisfaction. The following figure illustrates the major options available to a dissatisfied consumer.

Chart 3.4. Major Options Available to a Dissatisfied Consumer

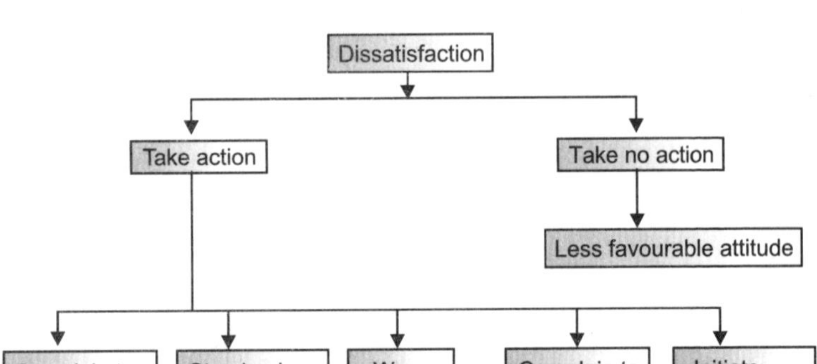

The dissatisfied consumer must first decide whether or not to take any external action. By taking no action the consumer decides to live with the unsatisfactory situation. An average of only one in three will make complaints.[9] This decision is a function of the importance of the purchase to the consumer, the ease of taking action, the consumer's existing level of overall satisfaction with the brand or outlet and the characteristics of the consumer involved. Even though no external action is taken, the consumer is likely to have a less favourable attitude toward the brand or store.

Consumers, who take action in response to dissatisfaction, may pursue one or more of the five alternatives.[10] These alternatives will damage the firm involved, both directly in terms of lost sales and indirectly in terms of a customer with a less favourable attitude.[11] So marketers should strive to minimise dissatisfaction and to effectively resolve dissatisfaction when it occurs.

These are the various steps in the process of consumer decision making which may vary depending upon the type of product and consumers involvement in the purchase.

REFERENCES

1. Hawkins I. Del et al., *Consumer Behaviour Building Marketing Strategy*, Tata McGraw Hill Publishing Company Limited, New Delhi, p. 562.
2. Ibid., p. 561.
3. Mark E. Slama et al., "Selected Socio-economic and Demographic Characteristics Associated with Purchasing Involvement", *Journal of Marketing*, Vol. 49, No. 1, Winter 1985, pp. 72-82.
4. Eric A. Greenleaf and Donald R. Lehmann, "Reasons for Substantial Delay in Decision Making", *Journal of Consumer Research,* Vol. 14, No. 1, June 1987, pp. 83-95.
5. Hill C.J., "The Nature of Problem Recognition and Search in the Extended Health Care Decision", *Journal of Services Marketing,* Vol. 15, No. 6 (2001), pp. 454-79.
6. Hawkins I. Del., *op.cit.*, p. 566.
7. Loudon L. David et al., *Consumer Behaviour*, McGraw Hill, Inc, New Delhi, 1983, p. 490.
8. Girish N. Punj and Richard Staelin, "A Model of Consumer Search Behaviour for New Automobiles", *Journal of Consumer Research*, Vol.9, No.4, 8 March 1983, pp. 366-380.
9. Newman Joseph, W., et al., IMR, Vol. IX, No. 3, August 1972.
10. Hays S., "Has Online Advertising Finally Grown Up?" *Advertising Age,* April 2002, p. 1.
11. Kasulis et al., "Validating the Retail Store Image Concept", *Journal of Marketing,* Vol.45, No.1, (Autumn 1981), pp. 119-135.
12. Robert A. West Brook, "Satisfaction/ Dissatisfaction in the Purchase Decision Process", *Journal of Marketing*, Vol. 42, No. 4, October 1978, p. 59.
13. Vikas Mittal et al., "Attribute Level, Performance, Satisfaction and Behavioural Intentions Over Time", *Journal of Marketing,* Vol. 63, No. 2, April 1999, pp. 88-101.
14. Rolph E. Anderson, "Consumer Dissatisfaction; The Effect of Discontinued Expectancy on Perceived Product Performance", *Journal of Marketing Research*, Vol. 11, No. 1, (February 1973), pp. 38-44.
15. Jagdip Singh, "Consumer Complaint Intentions and Behaviour; Definition and Taxonomical Issues", *Journal of Marketing*, Vol. 5, No. 1, (January 1988), pp. 93-107.
16. Singh J., "A Topology of Consumer Dissatisfaction Response Styles", *Journal of Retailing*, Spring 1990, pp. 57-97, cited in Del Hawkins et al., CB., New Delhi, Tata McGraw, p. 705.
17. Marsha Richins, "Negative Word of Mouth by Dissatisfied Consumers – A Pilot Study", *Journal of Marketing*, Vol. 47, No. 1, Winter 1983, pp. 68-78.

Buying Behaviour of Durable Goods

Introduction

Understanding the buying behaviour helps a firm seek better and effective ways to satisfy consumers, select advertising strategy and identify the target market. The key to an organisation's survival, profitability and growth in this highly competitive environment in the market is its ability to identify and satisfy unfulfilled consumer needs better and sooner than the competitors. This applies to durable goods also. In order to provide such an understanding, an attempt is being made in this chapter to examine certain aspects of buying behaviour in durable goods and the process of decision-making by the family.

This chapter comprises three parts. The first part presents the profile of the respondents. The second part provides details about the buying behaviour of the selected four durable goods. The last part deals with the process of decision making of durable goods by the family such as the reason for purchasing durable goods, the inducement factors, the factors related to store selection, the mode of purchase, the problems faced and the complaining behaviour of the respondents.

Profile of Sample Respondents

Four durable goods are chosen for the study and only those respondents who own all the four durable goods are selected for the study which includes 355 women respondents. The following tables show the demographic factors of the respondents and their family set up.

Age

Age is an important factor to have autonomy of decision making. Only married women above the age of 21 are selected for the study and women above the age of 60 are excluded.

Table 4.1: Age-wise Classification of Respondents

Sl. No.	Age	No. of Respondents	Percentage
1.	Below 30	87	24.5
2.	31–40	120	33.8
3.	Above 40	148	41.7
	Total	**355**	**100.0**

Source: Primary Data.

The table given above clearly shows that 42 per cent of the respondents are above the age of 40, 34 per cent in the age group of 31 to 40 while the remaining 24 per cent are young respondents below the age of 30. The average age of the respondents is 38.

Education

Education is directly related to purchasing power and it affects the decision-making process of the consumers. The education level of the respondents is shown below.

Table 4.2 : Education-wise Classification of Respondents

Sl. No.	Education Level	No. of Respondents	Percentage
1.	Below 12th	94	26.5
2.	Under Graduates (UG)	97	27.3
3.	Post Graduates (PG)	101	28.5
4.	Professional	63	17.7
	Total	**355**	**100.0**

Source: Primary Data.

From the table shown above it can be inferred that education level is evenly spread at all levels. Post Graduates are leading with 29 per cent and Under Graduates 27 per cent. School level respondents constitute 27 per cent while 18 per cent of the respondents are professionals.

Occupation

One's occupation provides status and income. The type of work one does directly influences one's values, lifestyle and all aspects of the consumption process.

Table 4.3 : Occupation-wise Classification of Respondents

Sl. No.	Occupation	No. of Respondents	Percentage
1.	Private Organisation	76	21.4
2.	Government Organisation	94	26.5
3.	Self employed	25	7.0
4.	Home makers	160	45.1
	Total	**355**	**100.0**

Source: Primary Data

It can be viewed from the table given above that 45 per cent of the respondents are unemployed, 27 per cent respondents working in government organisations, 21 per cent employed in private concerns and 7 per cent self employed.

Monthly Family Income

There is a direct correlation between income level and the purchasing power of a household. Marketers segment consumers on the basis of income and concentrate on the more affluent segments especially for the sale of durable goods.

Table 4.4 : Monthly Income-wise Classification of Respondents Family

Sl.No.	Income Level	No. of Respondents	Percentage
1.	Below Rs. 20000	223	62.8
2.	Rs. 20001 – Rs. 40000	82	23.1
3.	Above Rs. 40001	50	14.1
	Total	**355**	**100.0**

Source: Primary Data

The table given above shows that 63 per cent of the respondents have a family income below Rs. 20000 per month. 23 per cent earn Rs. 20001 to Rs. 40000 per month while only 14 per cent of the respondents have a family monthly income above Rs. 40001.

Religion

Religion may influence consumers in terms of seasonality of purchase guided by festival dates, which is a visible manifestation of influence on items of purchase and gifts. Religious codes restrict as well as guide consumption of different products.

Table 4.5 : Religion-wise Distribution of Respondents

Sl. No.	Religion	No. of	Percentage Respondents
1.	Hindus	124	34.8
2.	Christians	193	54.5
3.	Muslims	38	10.7
	Total	**355**	**100.0**

Source: Primary Data

The table given above shows that majority (55 per cent) of the respondents are Christians, 35 per cent Hindus, while the remaining 11 per cent Muslims.

Caste

Caste system is a deep-rooted factor in India. Caste too has an influence on the decision-making power in the family.

Table 4.6 : Caste-wise Distribution of Respondents

Sl. No.	Caste	No. of Respondents	Percentage
1.	Forward Caste	42	11.9
2.	Backward Caste	309	87.0
3.	Scheduled Caste	4	1.1
	Total	**355**	**100.0**

Source: Primary Data

The table presented above shows that 87 per cent of the respondents belong to Backward caste while 12 per cent Forward caste. Only 1.1 per cent belong to Scheduled caste.

Locality of Respondents

The purchasing and decision-making power of an individual may depend upon the locality to which they belong. So locality of the person is another important social factor that should be considered.

Table 4.7: Locality-wise Distribution of Respondents

Sl. No.	Locality	No. of Respondents	Percentage
1.	Urban	226	63.7
2.	Rural	129	36.3
	Total	**355**	**100.0**

Source: Primary Data

It can be known from the data given above that 64 per cent of the respondents are living in urban area and the remaining 36 per cent in rural area.

Size of the Family

Depending upon the type of the family and number of children the size of the family may vary which, in turn, influences the type and size of purchase of goods. Indian families are, in general, large in size.

Table 4.8 : Family Size-wise Distribution of Respondents

Sl. No.	Family Size	No. of Respondents	Percentage
1.	Upto 3 members	102	28.7
2.	4–5 members	235	66.2
3.	Above 5 members	18	5.1
	Total	**355**	**100.0**

Source: Primary Data

The table given above shows that 66 per cent of the respondents have a family size of 4 to 5 members, 29 per cent have just 3 members and only 5 per cent of the families have a membership of more than 5 members.

Number of Children

The purchasing power of the family depends upon the number of children in the family, their age and educational level.

Table 4.9 : Number of Children

Sl. No.	No. of Children	No. of Respondents	Percentage
1.	Upto 2	272	76.6
2.	Above 2	83	23.4
	Total	**355**	**100.0**

Source: Primary Data

It can be viewed from the table given above that 77 per cent of the respondents have a maximum of 2 children while only 23 per cent have more than 2 children.

Wealth Position

Indians have a disposition to save and preserve wealth by increasing their assets. Wealth plays an important role for purchasing and decision-making.

Table 4.10 : Wealth-wise Distribution of Respondents

Sl. No.	Wealth Position	No. of Respondents	Percentage
1.	Below Rs. 20 lakhs	250	70.4
2.	Above Rs. 20 lakhs	105	29.6
	Total	**355**	**100.0**

Source: Primary Data

The table presented above shows that 70 per cent of the respondents have wealth less than Rs. 20 lakhs worth and 30 per cent have more than Rs. 20 lakhs worth of properties.

Type of Family

In India both the nuclear and joint family systems prevail. The husband, the wife and the children constitute a nuclear family. The nuclear family together with atleast one grandparent is called an extended family. Joint family system is more commonly found in India than in other countries.

Table 4.11 : Type of Family-wise Distribution of Respondents

Sl. No.	Type of Family	No. of Respondents	Percentage
1.	Nuclear family	262	73.8
2.	Joint family	93	26.2
	Total	**355**	**100.0**

Source: Primary Data

It is clear from the table given above that 74 per cent of the respondents live in a nuclear type of family while the remaining 26 per cent in a joint family.

Ownership of Durable Goods

As this study is based on durable goods, some genuine information about the durable goods owned by the respondents and the brand preferences of durables owned by them are collected. The details are shown below.

Table 4.12 : Durable Goods Owned By Respondents

Sl. No.	Durables	No. of Respondents	Percentage
1.	Air Conditioner	67	18.9
2.	Car	168	47.3
3.	Computer	203	57.2
4.	DVD Player	294	82.8
5.	Grinder	342	96.4
6.	Micro Oven	95	26.8
7.	Mixie	355	100.0
8.	Mobile Phones	355	100.0
9.	Printer	57	16.1
10.	Vacuum Cleaner	81	22.8
11.	Water Purifier	92	25.9

Source: Primary Data.

The table given above clearly shows the ownership behaviour of durable goods of those who own Television, Refrigerator, Washing Machine and Two Wheeler. Only 18.9 per cent of these respondents own Air Conditioners and 47.3 per cent cars. 57.2 per cent of the respondents have computers for their personal use while 82.8 per cent DVD Players for entertainment.

Grinder is owned by 96.4 per cent of the respondents but microoven is owned only by 26.8 per cent of the respondents.

All the respondents have mixie and mobile phones for their family use. Printer is owned by only 16 per cent of the respondents. Only one fourth of the respondents own vacuum cleaner (23 per cent) for cleaning purpose and water purifier (26 per cent) for drinking pure and protected water.

Analysis of Brand Choice

Here are given the leading brands of the durable goods which are owned by the respondents in each of the durable goods.

This table 4.13 clearly shows that out of the respondents who own air conditioners, majority of them *i.e.,* 64 per cent have the brand 'LG'. The next leading Air Conditioner brand is 'Voltas'. Other brands are favoured by only a few of the respondents.

Among car owners, the leading brand is 'Maruti' which is owned by 72 per cent of the respondents. The next leading brand is 'Tata' which is owned by 10 per cent.

With regard to computer 60 per cent of the respondents use assembled computers. Only 40 per cent have Branded computers. The leading brand is HCL (12 per cent).

As regards DVD player the leading brand is 'SONY' owned by 54 per cent. Next is 'LG', which is owned by 10 per cent of the respondents.

Majority (35 per cent) of Grinder owners use 'Lekshmi' brand. Ultra model grinders are owned by 16 per cent of the respondents.

'LG' is the leading brand for microoven owned by 60 per cent of the respondents. The brand 'IFB' is owned by 16 per cent of the respondents.

As regards Mixie more than half (51 per cent) of the respondents use 'Preethi' brand. Next leading brand is 'Butterfly' owned by 17 per cent of the respondents.

Table 4.13 : Brand Preference of Durables

Sl. No.	Durables	Leading Brand I			Leading Brand II		
		Brand Name	No. of	Percentage Respondents	Brand Name	No. of	Percentage Respondents
1.	Air Conditioner	LG	43	64	Voltas	15	22
2.	Car	Maruthi	121	72	Tata	16	10
3.	Computer	Assembled	122	60	HCL	24	12
4.	DVD Player	Sony	158	54	LG	53	18
5.	Grinder	Lekshmi	125	35	Ultra	57	16
6.	Micro Oven	LG	57	60	IFB	15	16
7.	Mixie	Preethi	182	51	Butterfly	61	17
8.	Mobile Phones	Nokia	270	76	Sony Ericson	51	14
9.	Printer	HP	42	74	Epson	9	15
10.	Vacuum Cleaner	Euro Clean	61	75	Sony	8	10
11.	Water Purifier	Acqua Guard	90	98			

Source: Primary Data

'Nokia' is the most leading brand (76 per cent) in the case of mobile phones. Sony Ericson captures only 14 per cent.

With regard to Printer, 'HP' (74 per cent) is the most leading brand and the brand 'EPSON' captures 15 per cent of the printer market.

'Euroclean' is the leading brand regarding vacuum cleaners (75 per cent) and 'Sony' has just 10 per cent of the vacuum cleaner market.

As regards water purifier 'Aqua Guard' captures the total market

In general, it can be said that Multinational Companies Excel in the field of durable goods except in the case of Grinder and Mixie where Indian manufactures capture majority of the markets.

Buying Behaviour

Buying behaviour focuses on how individuals make decisions to spend their available resources on consumption. This includes what they buy, why they buy it, how much they buy, when they buy it, where they buy it and how they dispose it.

Buying Behaviour in Television

As one of the objectives is to study the buying behaviour, data are collected regarding the brand choice of Television, type of Television and the size of the Television owned by the respondents. These details are presented here.

Brand of Television

There are different brands of Television available in the market. Some are indigenously made while others manufactured by Multi national Companies.

This table 4.14 reveals the market share of the Television brand used by the respondents. The most widely used Television brand is 'Sony' used by 30.2 per cent of the respondents. The next popular brand is 'Onida' (19.7 per cent). 'LG' is used by 16.9 per cent of the respondents, 'Samsung' by 8.7 per cent of the respondents and 'BPL' by 8 per cent. Other brands like 'Videocon', 'Philips', 'National', 'AIWA' covers 17.7 per cent.

Table 4.14 : Choice of Television Brand

Sl. No.	Television	No. of Respondents	Percentage
1.	Sony	107	30.2
2.	Samsung	31	8.7
3.	Onida	70	19.7
4.	LG	60	16.9
5.	BPL	24	6.8
6.	Others	63	17.7
	Total	**355**	**100.0**

Source: Primary Data

This shows that Multinational brands are popular among the respondents.

Type of Television

There are many types of Television screens available. It may be a flat one, a projection type, a plasma type, an LCD type or an ordinary one.

Table 4.15 : Choice of Television Type

Sl. No.	Television Type	No. of Respondents	Percentage
1.	Ordinary	197	55.5
2.	Flat	113	31.8
3.	Projection	10	2.8
4.	LCD	26	7.3
5.	Plasma	9	2.6
	Total	**355**	**100.0**

Source: Primary Data

From the table given above it can be inferred that 55.5 per cent of the respondents use ordinary type of Television and 31.8 per cent own flat type Television. Only 2.8 per cent use projection type of Television and LCD type are owned by 7.3 per cent of the respondents. The new model, Plasma type, is owned by only 2.6 per cent of the respondents.

Screen Size of Television

The choice for the size of Television screens depends on the affluence and social status of the respondents.

Table 4.16 : Choice of Television Screen Size

Sl. No.	Screen Size	No. of Respondents	Percentage
1.	19″ and less than 19″	24	6.8
2.	20″	22	6.2
3.	21″	196	55.2
4.	24″	53	15.0
5.	More than 24″	60	16.8
	Total	**355**	**100.0**

Source: Primary Data

This table shows that 21 inch Television set is the most sought after size (55.2 per cent). The next size is 24 inches, owned by 15 per cent of the respondents. 20" screen size and less than that are chosen by 13 per cent while big size screen is preferred by 17 per cent of the respondents.

Buying Behaviour of Refrigerator

One of the products selected for the study is Refrigerator. So data are collected regarding the choice of brand, size, type of door and colour of the Refrigerator. The details are given below in the form of tables.

Brand of Refrigerator

There are many brands of Refrigerator available in the market which are manufactured by Multinational Companies and also by Indian companies. The table presented below gives the choice of brand of Refrigerator.

Table 4.17 : Choice of Brand of Refrigerator

Sl. No.	Refrigerator Brand	No. of Respondents	Percentage
1.	Whirlpool	109	30.7
2.	Samsung	16	4.5
3.	Godrej	54	15.2
4.	LG	100	28.2
5.	Kelvinator	28	7.9
6.	BPL	20	5.6
7.	Others	28	7.9
	Total	**355**	**100.0**

Source: Primary Data

This table shows the various brands of Refrigerator owned by the respondents. The most preferred brand is 'Whirlpool' which is being used by 30.7 per cent of the respondents. The next popular brand is 'LG' which is used by 28.2 per cent of the respondents. 15.2 per cent of the respondents prefer the brand 'Godrej' and 'Kelvinator' is owned by 7.9 per cent of the respondents. 'Samsung' Refrigerator is used by 4.5 per cent of the respondents while BPL is being used by 5.6 per cent of the respondents. Other brands cater to 7.9 per cent among the respondents. This shows that Multinational brands lead in the market of Refrigerator.

Type of Refrigerator Door

Refrigerators may be classified as single door, double door and more than 2 doors. Refrigerators having more than 2 doors are modern and recently introduced and are not popular among the respondents.

Table 4.18 : Choce of Door of Refrigerator

Sl. No.	Refrigerator Type	No. of Respondents	Percentage
1.	Double door	117	33.0
2.	Single door	238	67.0
	Total	**355**	**100.0**

Source: Primary Data

The table given above shows that 67 per cent of the respondents use single door Refrigerator only. Double door Refrigerator is owned by 33 per cent of the respondents while more than two doors are owned by only 2 respondents.

Colour of Refrigerator

Choice of colour of Refrigerator depends on one's taste. There are different colours of Refrigerators available in the market and their preference is presented in the table below.

Table 4.19 : Choice of Colour of Refrigerator

Sl. No.	Refrigerator Colour	No. of Respondents	Percentage
1.	Red	122	34.4
2.	White	55	15.5
3.	Grey	90	25.3
4.	Green	22	6.2
5.	Blue	60	16.9
6.	Others	6	1.7
	Total	**355**	**100.0**

Source: Primary Data

This table shows that 'Red' colour is the most sought after colour owned by 34.4 per cent of the respondents. Next choice goes to 'Grey' colour which is liked by 25.4 per cent of the respondents. The colour 'Blue' is preferred by 16.9 per cent while 'White' colour Refrigerator is owned by 15.5 per cent of the respondents. 'Green' colour is chosen by only 6.2 per cent of the respondents. While black, brown colours are favoured only by a meagre number of the respondents.

Size of Refrigerator

After fixing the brand and model of the Refrigerator, the consumers go for different sizes. The size preference of the respondents is given below.

The table 4.20 presented above clearly shows that the most preferred size of Refrigerator is 180 litres which is owned by 39 per cent of the respondents. Next choice goes to 165 litres which is owned by 29 per cent of the respondents. 215 litres is chosen by 12 per cent of the respondents and a very small size and a very big size are favoured by very few respondents.

Table 4.20 : Size Preference of Refrigerator

Sl. No.	Size	No. of Respondents	Percentage
1.	Less than 165 litres	4	1.13
2.	165 litres	104	29.30
3.	180 litres	138	38.87
4.	210 litres	32	9.01
5.	215 litres	42	11.83
6.	240 litres	26	7.32
7.	More than 240 litres	9	2.54
	Total	**355**	**100.00**

Source: Primary Data

Buying Behaviour in Washing Machine

In India Washing Machine has been introduced only recently but due to the change in economy, the socio-economic behaviour of women has changed to a greater extent which makes Washing Machine a necessary product in every home. The details are given below.

Brand of Washing Machine

Both multinational manufacturers and Indian producers try to capture the developing Indian women. The brand preference is shown below.

It is inferred from the table 4.21 shown above that the brand 'Whirlpool' leads the Washing Machine market by capturing 27.60 per cent of the respondents. The next leading brand is 'LG' owned by 22.3 per cent of the respondents. The brand 'IFB's share is 16 per cent and 'Videocon' captures 15 per cent. Other brands like 'Samsung', 'National' capture 20 per cent of the respondents.

Table 4.21 : Brand Preference of Washing Machine

Sl. No.	Brand	No. of Respondents	Percentage
1.	IFB	55	15.50
2.	Whirlpool	98	27.60
3.	Samsung	16	4.50
4.	LG	79	22.25
5.	Videocon	53	14.94
6.	Others	54	15.21
	Total	**355**	**100.0**

Source: Primary Data

Door of Washing Machine

The door of a Washing Machine may be placed at the top or in the front varying according to the model and brand of the Washing Machine.

Table 4.22 : Door Choice of Washing Machine

Sl. No.	Door Type	No. of Respondents	Percentage
1.	Top loading	274	77.2
2.	Front loading	81	22.8
	Total	**355**	**100.0**

Source: Primary Data

As per the table shown above 77.2 per cent of the respondents use top loading Washing Machine and 22.8 per cent of the respondents own front loading Washing Machine.

Type of Washing Machine

The Washing Machine may be fully automatic which will do all the functions automatically when switched on or semi automatic one. The details are given below.

Table 4.23 : Type of Washing Machine

Sl. No.	Type	No. of Respondents	Percentage
1.	Fully Automatic	186	52.4
2.	Semi Automatic	169	47.6
	Total	**355**	**100.0**

Source: Primary Data

This table shows that the respondents choose fully automatic Washing Machines (52.4 per cent) rather than semi automatic Washing Machines (47.6 per cent).

Size of Washing Machine

There are different sizes of Washing Machines available in the market. The details are in table 4.24.

Table No. 4.24 : Size of Washing Machine

Sl. No.	Size	No. of Respondents	Percentage
1.	Less than 4.5 litres	60	16.9
2.	5 litres	103	29.0
3.	5.5 litres	116	32.7
4.	6 litres	70	19.8
5.	More than 6 litres	6	1.6
	Total	**355**	**100.00**

Source: Primary Data

From the table 4.24 it is clear that majority (32.7 per cent) of the respondents prefer 5.5 litre size. 29 per cent of the respondents have 5 litre size. Small size (less than 4.5 litres) is owned by 17 per cent of the respondents while big size (6 litres and more) are used by nearly 20 per cent of the respondents.

Buying Behaviour in Two Wheelers

As one of the products chosen for the study is Two Wheeler, the details regarding the preference of brand, colour, capacity of Two Wheelers used both by the husband and the wife are gathered and presented here.

Ownership of Two Wheeler

Table 4.25 : Ownership of Two Wheeler Classification

Sl. No.	Owners	No. of Respondents	Percentage
1.	Husband	343	96.62
2.	Wife	86	24.2
3.	Both	12	3.38

Source: Primary Data

This table clearly shows that, in most of the families, 96.6 per cent of the husbands own their own Two Wheelers, and in a mere 3.4 per cent of the families, Two Wheelers are purchased to be used by both the spouses. Only one fourth (24.2 per cent) of the respondents have Two Wheelers for their own use. As very few families have Two Wheelers to be used by both the spouses the details regarding the brand, capacity and colour are included with the details of husband's Two Wheeler preference.

Husband's Choice of Brand of Two Wheeler

The brand details of the Two Wheeler a husband prefers are given below.

Table 4.26 : Husband's Choice of Brand of Two Wheelers

Sl. No.	Brand	No. of Respondents	Percentage
1.	Hero Honda	151	42.5
2.	TVS	98	27.6
3.	Bajaj	53	15.0
4.	Others	53	14.9
	Total	**355**	**100.0**

Source: Primary Data

This table 4.26 shows that in nearly 43 per cent of the families the husbands own the brand 'Hero Honda'. 'TVS' brand is owned by 28 per cent of the spouses. In 15 per cent of the families, the husbands have 'Bajaj' Two Wheelers. While other brands like 'Kinetic' (5 per cent), 'Pulsar' (3 per cent), 'Honda' (2.5 per cent) and 'Bullet' (3 per cent) capture 15 per cent of the market. Thus the leading brand among Two Wheelers is 'Hero Honda'.

Brand of Two Wheelers of Respondents

Only 24 per cent of the respondents have Two Wheelers for their own use and their brand preference is shown below.

From the table 4.27 it could be observed that 66.3 per cent of wives prefer 'TVS'. Next preference is for 'Kinetic' which is 16.3 per cent while the brand 'Honda' is the choice of 9.3 per cent of wives and other brands capture 8.1 per cent of female market .

Table 4.27 : Wives' Choice of Brand of Two Wheelers

Sl. No.	Brand	No. of Respondents	Percentage
1.	TVS	57	66.3
2.	Kinetic	14	16.3
3.	Honda	8	9.3
4.	Others	7	8.1
	Total	**86**	**100.0**

Source: Primary Data

Husband's Choice for Two Wheeler as regards its Capacity

The table below shows the Husband's Two Wheeler choice as regards its capacity.

Table 4.28 : Husbands Choice of Capacity of Two Wheeler

Sl. No.	CC	No. of Respondents	Percentage
1.	Less than 100	20	5.6
2.	100	235	66.2
3.	110	54	15.2
4.	150	32	9.0
5.	More than 150	14	4.0
	Total	**355**	**100.0**

Source: Primary Data

From the table shown above it is clear that majority (66 per cent) of the husbands choose 100 CC Two Wheelers and 15 per cent 110 CC. While other capacity Two Wheelers are not much in preference by husbands of the respondents.

Capacity Preference for Wives Two Wheeler

From table 4.29 it is clear that 62.8 per cent of wives like to own 60 CC Two Wheelers while 23.2 per cent have 100 CC. 14 per cent have 75 CC Two Wheelers.

Table. 4.29 : Wives Choice of Capacity in Two Wheeler

Sl. No.	CC	No. of Respondents	Percentage
1.	60	54	62.8
2.	75	12	14.0
3.	100	20	23.2
	Total	**86**	**100.0**

Source: Primary Data

Colour Choice of Two Wheelers

There are different colours of Two Wheelers available in the market. The following table shows the colour choice of Two Wheelers among husbands and wives.

Table 4.30 Colour Choice of Two Wheelers

Sl. No.	Colours	No. of Husbands	Percentage	No. of Wives	Percentage
1.	Black	214	60.2	55	64.0
2.	Red	44	12.4	8	9.3
3.	Grey	54	15.3	9	10.5
4.	Green	30	8.4	10	11.6
5.	Others	13	3.7	4	4.6
	Total	**355**	**100.0**	**86**	**100.0**

Source: Primary Data

This table 4.30 clearly shows the colour choice of the respondents for Two Wheelers. 'Black' is the most preferred colour by both husbands (60.2 per cent) and wives (64 per cent). Next choice is 'Grey' (15.3 per cent) by the husbands and 'Green' (11.6 per cent) by the wives. The colour 'Red' is favoured by 12.4 per cent of the husbands and 9.3 per cent of the wives. Other colours are not popular among the respondents.

Type of Purchase of Selected Durable Goods

Data are collected from the respondents to find out whether the durables they own are brand new ones or second hand. The details are given below:

Table 4.31 : Type of Durables Purchased

Sl. No.	Type	Televi-sion		Refrige-rator		Washing Machene		Two Wheeler	
		No.	(%)	No.	(%)	No.	(%)	No.	(%)
1.	Brand new	355	(100)	352	(99.2)	348	(98)	342	(96)
2.	Second hand	0	(0)	3	(.8)	7	(2)	13	(4)
	Total	**355**	**100**	**355**	**100**	**355**	**100**	**355**	**100**

Source: Primary Data

The table 4.31 shows that mostly all the respondents purchase brand new durable goods. Only 4 per cent of Two Wheeler owners have gone for second hand ones. In other words it can be said that second hand durables are not preferred to by the people.

Mode of Purchase of the Durable Goods

The durables can be purchased out of savings or from the money borrowed. If purchased by credit, they can buy the durables on instalment basis. The details are shown below.

Table 4.32 : Mode of Purchase of Durables

Sl. No.	Mode	Televi-sion		Refrige-rator		Washing Machene		Two Wheeler	
		No.	(%)	No.	(%)	No.	(%)	No.	(%)
1.	Savings	307	(86)	260	(73)	242	(68)	207	(58)
2.	Borrowed money	12	(4)	31	(9)	42	(12)	17	(5)
3.	Instalments	36	(10)	64	(18)	71	(20)	131	(37)
	Total	**355**	**(100)**	**355**	**(100)**	**355**	**(100)**	**355**	**(100)**

Source: Primary Data

This table 4.32 shows the mode of purchase of the durable goods by the respondents. It is clear that more than half of the respondents have purchased Refrigerator (73 per cent), Washing Machine (68 per cent), Two Wheelers (58 per cent) and Television (86 per cent) out of their own savings. Only a few respondents have made the purchase of durable goods out of borrowed money. Most of the Two Wheeler buyers do it on instalment basis.

Replacements of Products

Consumers have a number of options when a product is no longer useful to them or when they are tired of using the products. They may sell it, give it away, modify it and use it for some other purpose, exchange it with the next purchase or dispose it as trash. The table given below shows how the respondents replace their durables under study.

Table 4.33 : Replacement Behaviour

Sl. No.	Type of Replacement	Television		Refrigerator		Washing Machene		Two Wheeler	
		No.	(%)	No.	(%)	No.	(%)	No.	(%)
1.	Sold	74	(32)	46	(23)	32	(22)	76	(31)
2.	Exchanged	123	(52)	128	(63)	82	(56)	152	(62)
3.	Gifted	15	(7)	19	(90	24	(17)	8	(3)
4.	Using for some other purpose	14	(6)	8	(4)	4	(3)	9	(4)
5.	Thrown to garbage	8	(3)	2	(1)	3	(2)	0	(0)
	Total	**234**	**(100)**	**203**	**(100)**	**145**	**(100)**	**245**	**(100)**

Source: Primary Data

This table clearly shows the replacement behaviour of the respondents with regard to the selected goods. 32 per cent of the Television owners have sold them, more than half of the respondents *i.e.* 52 per cent have exchanged it for a new one and only a few respondents have gifted or treated it as a waste or used it for buying something else. As regards Refrigerator the same behaviour is seen as 63 per cent have exchanged their old products for replacement and 23 per cent sold their Refrigerator to replace it with a new one.

As regards Washing Machine 56 per cent of the respondents have exchanged their old ones for new ones while 22 per cent sold their worn out Washing Machine for replacement.

The replacement behaviour of the respondents with regard to Two Wheelers is that 62 per cent of the respondents exchange their old Two Wheeler and 28 per cent have sold their old Two Wheelers in order to purchase a new one.

Process of Family Purchase Decision

The process which the family members go through before, during and after making a purchase helps the marketers know about the consumer behaviour. It begins with knowing the reason for buying a product, then searching some kind of information about the product and critically evaluating to choose an alternative brand. Finally, selecting a store for the purchase and evaluating and experiencing the outcome of the purchase decision are made.

Reasons for Buying Durable Goods

Durable goods are those goods which cost more, less frequently purchased and used for a longer period. As this study relates to the purchase of durable goods, the respondents are asked to rank the reasons for buying the durable items. Eight reasons are given. "*Henry's Garrett Ranking Principle*" has been applied to find out the reasons for buying the durable goods. The order of merit thus given by the respondents for the eight reasons is converted into ranks by using the formula

$$\text{Present Position} = \frac{100(R - 0.50)}{N}$$

Where R: Rank given by the respondents

N: Number of factors *i.e.*, 8.

The ranks thus obtained are converted into scores with the help of Garrett's table (Appendix-II). For each reason, the scores of individual respondents are added together and divided by the total number of respondents. The mean scores for all the reasons are arranged in the ascending order and ranks are given in the order of importance.

It is inferred from the table 4.34 that the main reason for purchasing the durable goods is 'Necessity' which has scored the highest. The second reason for buying the durables is for 'Comfort and Convenience'. The third reason being 'To Save Time'. 'To maintain economy' and 'to avoid unnecessary expenditure' are the fourth and fifth in the order of rank. The last rank scored is for increasing asset

Table 4.34 : Reason for Purchasing Durables

Sl. No.	Reasons	Mean Scores	Rank
1.	Necessity	71.16	1
2.	Comfort and convenience	57.28	2
3.	To save time	53.35	3
4.	To maintain economy	49.71	4
5.	To avoid unnecessary expenditure	49.16	5
6.	To gain knowledge	43.7	6
7.	Social status	40.78	7
8.	To increase asset	35.86	8

Sources of Searching Information

After the consumer decides that the shortages or unfulfilled desires are worth further consideration, information is gathered. Information search requires the assembly of a list of alternate products and a determination of the characteristics of each alternative. The consumer collects data about the products that are most likely to solve their problem. Information search may involve commercial sources, non-commercial sources and social sources. This process depends upon the experience of the consumer and the level of perceived risk. Marketers are interested in knowing from which source the consumers are collecting information about the product to decide the sales promotion strategy and to plan the messages to be conveyed in advertisement.

Table 4.35 : Sources of Gathering Information

Sl. No.	Products	Oral Advertisement	Printing Advertisement	Social Sources	Modern Technology
1.	Television	122 (34.4)	170 (47.9)	243 (68.5)	12 (3.4)
2.	Refrigerator	135 (38.0)	148 (41.7)	206 (58.0)	8 (2.2)
3.	Washing Machine	126 (35.5)	116 (32.7)	238 (67.0)	6 (1.7)
4.	Two Wheeler	72 (20.3)	136 (38.3)	384(108.2)	9 (2.5)

Note: Values in parenthesis is given in percentages. It may exceed 100 per cent as the respondent has the option of choosing any number of given sources

Source: Primary Data

The above table 4.35 clearly shows that social classes such as family members, friends and colleagues and printing advertisements such as newspaper, magazine and catalog play a vital role still today in supplying information about the product to the respondents more than the modern technologies like internet, e-mail and mobile advertisements.

As regards Television, both the social source (69 per cent) and the printing (48 per cent) advertisement give a fair amount of knowledge about the product. For Refrigerator, oral (34 per cent), printing (42 per cent) and social class (58 per cent) play an important role in providing information about the product. For Washing Machine, oral advertisement (36 per cent) such as Radio and Television advertisement supply more knowledge than printing advertisement (33 per cent), and social classes (67 per cent) plays an important role in providing information for their purchase. Social classes (108.2 per cent) provide information about Two Wheeler more than other types of oral (20 per cent) or printing advertisement (38 per cent).

Among women respondents modern technology plays a minimum role in providing information on durable goods.

Evaluating Brands

Once information is acquired, it will be processed by using short-term and long-term memory. Short-term memory acts as a filter to determine the information that is retained in long-term memory. Information stored in long-term memory is organised into schemes which represent the sets of associations consumers have with brands, products or companies. Such schemas are the basis for brand or company images. Consumers retrieve information from long-term memory to evaluate brands.

The respondents are asked to rank the factors that are considered for buying the brand of the selected durables. 'Garrett ranking technique' is used to find the most influential variable in deciding the brand they are using.

Table 4.36 : The Inducement Factors

Sl. No.	Variables	Television		Refrigerator		Washing Machine		Two Wheeler	
		Mean Score	Rank	Mean Score	Rank	Mean Score	Rank	Mean Score	Rank
1.	Advertisement	59.8	II	57.0	II	59.5	I	57.2	II
2.	Previous experience	53.7	IV	50.8	III	50.8	VI	57.9	I
3.	Friends	53.1	V	59.0	I	54.5	III	56.5	III
4.	Relatives	60.1	I	50.7	IV	52.7	IV	52.5	V
5.	Goodwill of Manufacturer	48.5	VI	48.6	V	51.0	V	52.0	VI
6.	Reputation of Retailer	36.8	VII	46.4	VII	40.2	VII	42.2	VII
7.	Retailers recommendation	33.9	VIII	42.2	VIII	33.9	VIII	35.6	VIII
8.	Family members	55.1	III	46.5	VI	58.5	II	53.9	IV

From the table 4.36 it is clear that the inducement factor differs from product to product. Advertisement plays a very influential factor in deciding the brand for all the products selected for the study. Advertisement factor has scored the first rank for Washing Machine and the second rank for other durables. Previous experience also plays a significant role in the purchase decision for durables especially for Two Wheeler, for which this variable scores the first rank. For Television and Washing Machine, it has scored the fourth rank and for Refrigerator the third rank.

Friends are also another important inducement factor for the purchase of durables. It has scored the first rank as regards Refrigerator but for Washing Machine and Two Wheeler it scores the third rank. Friends have less influence for the purchase of Television.

The factor 'Relatives' plays an important role for the inducement of purchase of Television as its mean score is the highest. But for other durables, it is the medium inducement factor.

Goodwill of the manufacturer also plays an inducement factor in deciding the brand of durables to be purchased as it scores fourth or fifth rank.

Reputation of retailer and retailer's recommendation about the brand are the least inducement factors for making purchase decision of durables as these variables score seventh and eighth position for each durable.

The wish of the family members is another important inducement factor in deciding the brand to be purchased. It plays an important role for Washing Machine, for which this variable has scored the second rank and for Television, the third rank. For Refrigerator and Two Wheeler it plays only a medium role in deciding the brand.

Factors Influencing the Purchase Decision of Selected Durable Goods

Before making the decision for the purchase of goods different factors are considered, especially for taking purchase decision of highly involved durable goods as it costs more, less frequently purchased and have a longer shelf life. Marketers should know the factors that are considered by customers while making purchase decision to design the marketing mix.

In order to highlight the most and least influential factors, the Likert Scale developed by Rensis Likert is used for each product. The respondents are asked to agree or disagree with 12 factors and each response is given a numerical score—5 for strongly agree, 4 for agree, 3 for no opinion, 2 for disagree and 1 for strongly disagree, to reflect the degree of attitudinal favourableness and the scores are summed up to measure the participants over all attitude.

The table 4.37 gives the comparative scoring ranks of the selected durable goods.

The table 4.37 clearly shows the comparative study on the factors influencing the purchase decision of the selected durables. The most important factor considered is 'Performance' of the durables as it scores the maximum for all the durable goods under study. The factor 'durability' scores second rank in the case of Television, fourth rank for Refrigerator and Washing Machine and fifth rank for Two Wheeler. 'Guarantee' given by the manufacturer is considered as second in importance in the case of Washing Machine but it got third rank for Television and Refrigerator and fourth rank for Two Wheeler. 'Brand name' is also another important factor as it got third rank for Washing Machine and Two Wheeler and fourth rank in the purchase of Television and Refrigerator. 'Price' has scored the second rank for Refrigerator and Two Wheeler but it got fifth rank for Television and Washing Machine. The factors 'popularity', 'discount offer' and 'neighbours envy' are the least important factors considered for the purchase of durable goods as they score the lowest for all the selected durable goods.

These factors should be considered by the manufacturers while planning and designing the advertisement strategy for each durable goods.

Table 4.37 : Factors Influencing the Purchase of Selected Goods

Sl. No.	Factors	Television		Refrigerator		Washing Machine		Two Wheeler	
		Score	Rank	Score	Rank	Score	Rank	Score	Rank
1.	Performance	1573	I	1573	I	1558	I	1570	I
2.	Durability	1539	II	1485	VI	1479	IV	1481	V
3.	Guarantee	1522	III	1554	III	1551	II	1513	IV
4.	Brand name	1519	IV	1532	IV	1488	III	1521	III
5.	Price	1477	V	1555	II	1477	V	1547	II
6.	Colour	1456	VI	1414	IX	1406	VIII	1467	VI
7.	Design	1452	VII	1452	VII	1446	VI	1452	VIII
8.	Availability of spare parts	1442	VIII	1522	V	1401	IX	1442	IX
9.	Model	1428	IX	1433	VIII	1408	VII	1463	VII
10.	Popularity	1336	X	1365	X	1350	X	1407	X
11.	Discount offer	1183	XI	1170	XI	1215	XI	1149	XI
12.	Neighbours envy	983	XII	926	XII	922	XII	928	XII

Source: Computed from Primary Data

Factor Analysis

The marketing manager is shooting in the dark, trying to figure out what really drives buyer behaviour and what are the underlying significant drives of behaviour. Factor Analysis is a good way of resolving this confusion and identifying latent or underlying factors from an array of seemingly important variables.

The technique of Factor Analysis is used to reduce the number of variables into a smaller and manageable number by combining related ones into factors. 'Principal Component Analysis' method is used to extract factors with an Eigen Value of 1 or more. In order to assign variables 'Rotated Factor Matrix' is used.

In this study Factor Analysis is applied for the factors influencing the purchase of all the selected durable goods and the results are given one by one.

1. Television : In order to find the appropriateness of this analysis Kaiser Meyer Olkin (KMO) and Bartlett's Test of Sphericity is used and the results are shown below.

Table 4.38 : KMO and Bartlett's Test

KMO Measure of sampling adequacy	.621
Bartlett's test of Sphericity	
App. Chi-square value	760.523
df	66
Sig.	.000

The KMO value is very high (.621). Similarly, the Bartlett's test rejects the null hypothesis *i.e.,* the variables are not related as the approximate chi-square value is 760.523 at 66 degrees of freedom which is significant at 1 per cent level of significance. Thus factor analysis may be considered as an appropriate technique.

The results of Principal Component Analysis to extract the number of variables are given below:

Table 4.39 : Principal Component Analysis

Component	Extraction Sums of Squared Loading			Rotated Sums of Squared Loading		
	Total	Percentage of Variables	Cumulative Percentage	Total	Percentage of Variables	Cumulative Percentage
1.	2.749	22.906	22.906	2.355	19.627	19.627
2.	1.721	14.344	37.251	1.806	15.050	34.677
3.	1.385	11.542	48.792	1.627	13.557	48.234
4.	1.090	9.082	57.875	1.157	9.641	57.875

From the table shown above it is clear that 4 factors can be extracted together which account for 57.88 per cent of the total 12 variables. Hence 12 factors are summated to 4 factors by loosing nearly 42 per cent of data.

The table presented below gives the Rotated Component Matrix table found by using Varimax Method which is used to assign factors which have higher loadings.

Table 4.40 : Rotated Component Matrix

Sl. No.	Factors	Product Features	Product Function	Sales Strategy	Brand Equity
1.	Colour	.758			
2.	Design	.746			
3.	Model	.678			
4.	Popularity	.646			
5.	Performance		.740		
6.	Availability of spares		.666		
7.	Durability		.659		
8.	Discount offer			.836	
9.	Gurantee			.561	
10.	Neighbours envy			.574	
11.	Brand name				.908

The table 4.40 clearly shows that in the first column the variables namely 'Colour', 'Design', 'Model' and 'Popularity' have higher loadings of .758, .746, .678 and .646 respectively and it can be suggested that factor 1 is the combination of these four factors and have the variance of 19.627 per cent and it can be named as 'Product Features'.

From the second column it can be seen that the variables of 'Performance', 'Availability of Spare Parts' and 'Durability' have higher loadings with a variance of 15.050 and it can be combined and called as 'Product Functioning'.

The third column shows that the factors 'Discount Offer' .836, 'Guarantee' .561 and 'Neighbours Envy' .574 have high loadings and are summated and named as 'Sales Strategy'.

In the last column only one variable *i.e.,* the 'Brand Name' has the higher loading to be named as 'Brand Equity'.

Thus 12 factors are reduced to four variables and are given different names by using factor analysis. Thus 'product features', 'product functioning', 'sales stråtegy' and 'brand equity' are the factors influencing the purchase of Television.

2. Refrigerator : KMO measures of sampling adequacy and Bartlett's test of Sphericity to test the appropriateness of factor model is made and the result is shown below.

Table 4.41 : KMO and Bartlett's Test

KMO Measure of sampling adequacy	.811
Bartlett's test of Sphericity	
App. Chi-square value	3000.913
df	36
Sig.	.000

The KMO and Bartlett's test shows a green signal for factor analysis as KMO value is very high and chi-square value rejects the null hypothesis at 99 per cent confidence level.

The following table 4.42 shows the result of Principal Component Analysis to find out the number of variables with an Eigen value more than 1.

Table 4.42 : Principal Component Analysis

Component	Extraction Sums of Squared Loading			Rotated Sums of Squared Loading		
	Total	Percentage of Variables	Cumulative Percentage	Total	Percentage of Variables	Cumulative Percentage
1.	4.644	38.702	38.702	2.920	24.335	24.335
2.	1.478	12.318	51.020	2.821	23.512	47.846
3.	1.229	10.244	61.265	1.610	13.418	61.265

From the 4.42 above it can be inferred that three factors can be extracted together which accounts for 61.3 per cent out of the 12 variables. So 38.7 per cent of data are lost and twelve variables are minimised to three factors.

Table 4.43 : Rotated Component Matrix

Sl. No.	Factors	Operational Influence	Physical Features	Sales Strategy
1.	Performance	.730		
2.	Guarantee	.772		
3.	Availability of spare parts	.781		
4.	Durability	.670		
5.	Brand name		.688	
6.	Colour		.787	
7.	Design		.808	
8.	Model		.611	
9.	Discount offer			.506
10.	Neighbours envy			.849
11.	Popularity			.593

The three variables and their combination can be assessed from the table presented above. For factor one, the variables of 'Performance', 'Guarantee', 'Availability of Spare Parts' and 'Durability' with higher loadings can be combined together and are named as "Operational Influence".

The next four factors of 'Brand Name', 'Colour', 'Design' and 'Model' have higher loadings in the second column and are given the name 'Physical Features'.

The third factor namely 'Discount Offer', 'Neighbours Envy' and 'Popularity' are combined together to be called as 'Sales Strategy'.

These three factors can be used to design communication or marketing strategy for Refrigerator. From this it can be inferred that the factors 'Operational Influence', 'Physical Features' and 'Sales Strategy' will influence the family to purchase Refrigerator.

3. Washing Machine : The result of testing the factor model of KMO test and Bartlett's test is shown below.

Table 4.44 : KMO and Bartlett's Test

KMO Measure of sampling adequacy	0.501
Bartlett's test of Sphericity	
App. Chi-square value	629.711
df	66
Sig.	0.000

These tests give a green signal for factor analysis.

The findings of the Principal Component Analysis which is used to extract the number of variables by using the Eigen Value above 1 is given below.

Table 4.45 : Principal Component Analysis-Variance Explained

Component	Extraction Sums of Squared Loading			Rotated Sums of Squared Loading		
	Total	Percentage of Variables	Cumulative Percentage	Total	Percentage of Variables	Cumulative Percentage
1.	2.398	19.982	19.982	1.825	15.212	15.212
2.	1.502	12.519	32.501	1.700	14.163	29.375
3.	1.477	12.312	44.813	1.552	12.936	42.311
4.	1.193	9.944	54.757	1.317	10.973	53.285
5.	1.131	9.424	64.181	1.308	10.896	64.181

Five variables can be extracted which amount to a cumulative percentage of 64.2 per cent loosing the remaining 35.8 per cent of data can be inferred from the table shown above. Thus five factors which influence the purchase of Washing Machine are extracted from 12 factors.

Table 4.46 : Rotated Component Matrix

Sl. No.	Factors	Fringe Benefits	Brand Belief	Physical Features	Brand Image	Dealer Support
1.	Performance	.766				
2.	Guarantee	.736				
3.	Price	.597				
4.	Durability		.813			
5.	Model		.613			
6.	Brand		.643			
7.	Design			.878		
8.	Colour			.704		
9.	Neighbours Envy				.797	
10.	Popularity				.565	
11.	Discount Offer					.845
12.	Availability of Spare Parts					.552

This table clearly shows the important factors considered for the purchase of Washing Machine. The first factor is the combination of the variables with high factor loadings of .766 for 'Performance', .736 for 'Guarantee' and .597 for 'Price' and are named as "Fringe Benefit".

The next three factors of 'Durability' with a loading of .813, 'Model' .613 and 'Brand' having a loading of .643 are combined together and named as "Brand Belief". This is factor two.

The third factor is the combination of 'Design' (.878) and 'Colour' (.704) and its percentage of variance is 14.163 which can be called as "Physical Features".

The variables "Neighbours Envy" with a loading of .797 and 'Popularity' with a loading of .565 can be combined and named as "Brand Image".

In the last loading column the factors 'Discount Offer' with a loading of .845 and 'Availability of Spare Parts' with a loading of .552 are combined together with a percentage of variance of 10.896 which can be called as 'Dealer Support'.

Thus it can be concluded that 'Fringe Benefit', 'Brand Belief', 'Physical Features', 'Brand Image' and 'Dealer Support' are the main factors influencing the purchase of Washing Machine and by using factor analysis 12, variables are reduced to five variables. These factors can be used in advertising strategy for Washing Machine.

4. Two Wheeler : The findings of Kaiser-Meyer-Olkin Test and Bartlett's test of Sphericity are given below.

Table 4.47 : KMO and Bartlett's Test

KMO Measure of sampling adequacy	0.674
Bartlett's test of Sphericity	
App. Chi-square value	774.442
df	66
Sig.	0.000

As the KMO value is high (.674) and chi-square test rejects the null hypothesis at 1 per cent significance level, Factor Analysis can be considered as a good model.

The Principal Component Analysis is used to find out the number of variables to be extracted and its findings are shown below.

Table 4.48 : Principal Component Analysis—Variance Explained

Component	Extraction Sums of Squared Loading			Rotated Sums of Squared Loading		
	Total	Percentage of Variables	Cumulative Percentage	Total	Percentage of Variables	Cumulative Percentage
1.	2.795	23.292	23.292	2.126	17.720	17.720
2.	1.862	15.518	38.810	1.950	16.249	33.969
3.	1.341	11.171	49.981	1.577	13.138	47.106
4.	1.089	9.073	59.054	1.434	11.948	59.054

From this table it can be understood that Four variables can be extracted which have a Eigen Value of 1 or greater than 1. These four variables account for 59.054.

The Varimax Analysis with Kaiser Rotation is carried out on 12 factors influencing the purchase of Two Wheeler.

Table 4.49 : Rotated Component Matrix

Sl.	Factors	Physical Features	Product Reliability	Value Equity	Emotional Influence
1.	Design	.753			
2.	Colour	.710			
3.	Brand	.660			
4.	Model	.593			
5.	Durability		.778		
6.	Performance		.724		
7.	Availability of Spare Parts		.611		
8.	Price			.746	
9.	Guarantee			.625	
10.	Popularity			.504	
11.	Discount Offer				.753
12.	Neighbours Envy				.791

It can be inferred that four factors can be extracted according to its importance in influencing the purchase of Two Wheelers out of twelve variables.

'Physical Features' has the variance of 17.720 and in this factor 'Design' of Two Wheeler has a high factor loading of 0.753, followed by 'Colour' .710, 'Brand' .660 and 'Model' .593.

The next factor considered is 'Product Reliability' which has a percentage of variance of 16.249 and is a combination of 'Durability' (.778), 'Performance' (.724) and 'Availability of Spare Parts' (.611).

From the third factor column it can be viewed that the variables 'Price', 'Guarantee' and 'Popularity' have higher loadings with a variance of 13.138 and it can be combined and named as 'Value Equity'.

In the last column, two variables of 'Discount Offer' and 'Neighbours Envy' account for 11.943 with a loading of .753 and .791 respectively which are named as'Emotional Influence'.

Thus by using data reduction analysis twelve factors are minimised to four factors which are called as 'Physical

Features', 'Product Reliability', 'Value Equity' and 'Emotional Influence'. These are the factors influencing the purchase of Two Wheeler which can be used by Two Wheeler manufacturers and dealers while designing the advertisement strategy.

Reason for Store Selection

Of the different options available to the customer to buy the product, they will pick and choose only one store. Selecting a particular shop to purchase the goods may be due to various reasons. The respondents are asked to rank the eleven variables which are considered for store selection. "*Garrett Ranking Technique*" is applied to find the most and least important reasons for selecting a particular shop.

Table 4.50 : Reasons for Store Selection

Sl. No.	Variable No.	Grand Mean Score	Rank
1.	Goodwill	59.61	1
2.	Good after sales service	58.66	2
3.	Price offer	55.35	3
4.	More choices	54.02	4
5.	Convenience	53.83	5
6.	Own experience	51.1	6
7.	Dealers opinion	46.2	7
8.	Credit facility	45.44	8
9.	Friends / relatives recommendation	45.2	9
10.	Showroom	42.14	10
11.	Less formality	40.3	11

From the table given above it can be inferred that 'goodwill' is the main factor considered for selecting a particular store for purchasing durable goods. The second rank scored is for 'good after sales service'. The consumers are price conscious as 'price offer facility' scores the third rank and 'more choices' in the shop get the fourth rank. 'Convenience in location' is another important factor considered for the selection of a store. Showroom and less formality in purchase are the least important factors considered for selecting stores.

Problems Faced in Purchase Decision of Durable Goods

A customer may face many problems in the post purchase of durable goods. In order to know the problems faced, the respondents are given 13 options of which they have the option to choose any number of problems. These problems are divided into three, namely financial problems, mental problems and marketing problems. 'Financial problems' includes problems relating to over investment, unnecessary

Table 4.51 : Problems Faced at the Purchase of Durables

Sl. No.	Problems	Number of Respondents	Percentage
I	**Marketing Problems**		
1.	Misleading advertisement	137	38.6
2.	Poor aftersales service	74	20.8
3.	Wrong information	72	20.3
4.	Cheating by dealers	42	11.8
II	**Financial Problems**		
1.	Over maintenance	77	21.7
2.	Over investment	39	11.0
3.	Unnecessary payment of interest	36	10.1
4.	Unnecessary investment	35	9.9
III	**Mental Problems**		
1.	Decision without enquiry	49	13.8
2.	Not necessary	26	7.3
3.	Wrong decision	14	3.9
4.	Undue burden	11	3.1

Source: Primary data

investment, unnecessary payment of interest, credit purchase and over maintenance expenses. 'Mental problems' includes wrong decision of purchase, purchasing durables which are not necessary, decided on the purchase without adequate enquiry and undue burden. The 'Marketing problems' are cheating by dealers, misleading advertisements, poor after sales service and providing wrong information about the product.

It can be inferred from the table 4.51 that one of the main problems faced by the respondents while making the purchase decision is marketing problem in which misleading advertisement (38.6 per cent) is the leading problem and this should be made a note of by the marketers. Next vital marketing problem faced by respondents is poor after sales service (20.8 per cent) and providing wrong information (20.3 per cent) by marketers. Cheating by dealers is another problem (11.8 per cent).

Next leading problem faced by the respondents is financial problem. Here, over maintenance expenses (21.7 per cent) is mainly faced by the respondents during the purchase of durable goods. Over investment (11 per cent), unnecessary payment of interest (10.1 per cent) and unnecessary investment (9.9 per cent) are the other financial problems faced by the respondents.

Regarding the mental problems faced, decision taken without proper enquiry (13.8 per cent) is the major problem which is avoidable. Other problems like purchase is not necessary (7.3 per cent), wrong decision (3.9 per cent) and undue burden (3.1 per cent) are not big ones.

Marketers should view these problems seriously and care should be taken to reduce unfair trade practices in order to satisfy the customers and earn goodwill among them to survive and flourish in this competitive world.

Effects on Consumer Dissatisfaction

Long before the consumers make the final purchase, they build up an expectation about the desired products with regard to the benefits they will provide and the needs they should fulfill. The moment a product is purchased and used, they begin to judge it. The level of satisfaction or dissatisfaction they experience depends upon how well the product's performance meets their expectations. If the performance of the product falls short of their expectations there will be dissatisfaction. Marketers should match product benefits with consumer needs by narrowing the gap between expectation and performance.

Not all consumers who are dissatisfied with the performance of a purchase take steps to remedy the situation. The complaining behaviour can take three paths *i.e.,* no action, public action and private action.

Chart 4.1 : Effects of Consumer Dissatisfaction

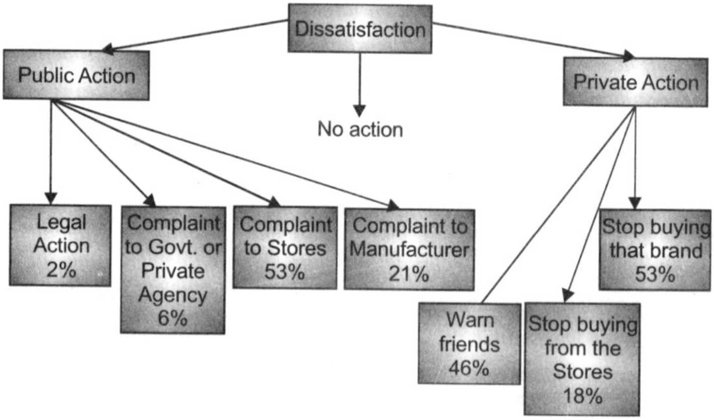

Dissatisfaction
Public Action
No action
Private Action
Legal Action 2%
Complaint to Govt. or Private Agency 6%
Complaint to Stores 53%
Complaint to Manufacturer 21%
Warn friends 46%
Stop buying from the Stores 18%
Stop buying that brand 53%

Source: Percentage will exceed 100 per cent as respondent may opt one or more actions.

Each dissatisfied respondent can take no action, public action and/or private action. From this model it can be inferred that more than half (53 per cent) of the respondents prefer to take public action of complaining to the stores from where the durables are purchased. The same percentage of the respondents take private reaction by stop buying that brand. 46 per cent are of the opinion that they will warn their friends about buying the products. Only a few customers will take to legal action or report to the government or approach a private redressal forum.

Conclusion

This chapter presents a clear view of the profile of the respondents giving details about the demographic factors of age, income, occupation, education, area of residence, number of children, family size, wealth position and the type of family. Also it explains the buying behaviour of the respondents regarding their brand choice, size, colour for each product chosen for the study and details about the ownership of all the durable goods owned by the respondents. The last part of this chapter explains the process of decision making by the family, the reason for buying the durable goods, inducement factors, factors influencing the purchase of durable goods and store selection and the problems faced by the respondents besides the complaining behaviour of the respondents.

CHAPTER 5

Role of Women in the Decision-Making Process of Family Purchase

Introduction

Family is the basic consumer decision-making unit in which each member plays a significant role. Marketers examine the attitude and behaviour of the member of the family whom they believe is to be the major decision maker. They have to determine who in the family plays which role before they can affect the family decision process. Each member may play a different role for different product decisions. This will help them decide the communication message for advertising strategy.

As one of the objectives of the study is to make a comparative study of the role of women in family purchase decisions for the selected goods, in this chapter, each one's role is presented in tabular form and analysed with the help of chi-square test to find out the relationship between the role of family members and the demographic factors of area of residence and employment of women.

Initiator

The family member who first recognises a need and starts the process decision making for a purchase can be called an initiator. Table 5.1 shows each of the family member's role as an initiator for the selected durables.

The table 5.1 clearly shows the role of family members as initiators. As regards the purchase of Television (53 per cent) and Two Wheeler (72 per cent) husband is the main initiator. Wife's role as an initiator is mainly for the products of Refrigerator (55 per cent) and Washing Machine (57 per cent). Children and others do not play a significant role as initiators for the purchase of the selected durables. Similarly, the joint initiation role of husband and wife is also worthy of consideration for the purchase of durable goods.

Table 5.1 : Role Structure as an Initiator

Sl. No.	Initiator	Television	Refrigerator	Washing Machine	Two Wheeler
1.	Husband	187 (52.7)	89 (25.1)	64 (18.0)	254 (71.6)
2.	Wife	34 (9.5)	196 (55.2)	201 (56.6)	23 (6.5)
3.	Husband and wife	68 (19.2)	57 (16.1)	60 (16.9)	38 (10.7)
4.	Children	61 (17.2)	3 (0.8)	6 (1.7)	31 (8.7)
5.	Others	5 (1.4)	10 (2.8)	24 (6.8)	9 (2.5)
	Total	**355 (100.0)**	**355 (100.0)**	**355 (100.0)**	**355 (100.0)**

Note: Data in Parenthesis is Percentage
Source: Primary Data

Influencer

The member of the family who, with expertise and interest in a particular purchase, gathers and provides information to other members about a product can be called an influencer. The role of the family member who influences others is given in the Table 5.2.

It can be inferred from the table 5.2 that husband is the main influencer for all the selected durables. His role as provider of information is mainly for the products Television (54 per cent) and Two Wheeler (63 per cent) while wife is a gatherer of information for the products of Refrigerator (38 per cent) and Washing Machine (49 per cent). For these products too the husband's role is noteworthy and others play only a small role as information gatherers and providers.

Table 5.2 : Influencer's Role in Family

Sl. No.	Influencers	Television	Refrigerator	Washing Machine	Two Wheeler
1.	Husband	190 (53.5)	129 (36.3)	118 (33.2)	223 (62.8)
2.	Wife	79 (22.3)	133 (37.5)	159 (44.8)	47 (13.2)
3.	Jointly	29 (8.2)	28 (7.9)	25 (7.0)	30 (8.5)
4.	Children	35 (9.8)	26 (7.3)	20 (5.7)	43 (12.1)
5.	Others	22 (6.2)	39 (11.0)	33 (9.3)	12 (3.4)
	Total	**355 (100.0)**	**355 (100.0)**	**355 (100.0)**	**355 (100.0)**

Note: Data in Parenthesis is Percentage
Source: Primary Data

Motivator

Motivator is a person who encourages other members of the family to buy the product that are under consideration. She acts as an accelerator in making the purchase decision.

Table 5.3 : Role Structure as Motivators

Sl. No.	Motivators	Television	Refrigerator	Washing Machine	Two Wheeler
1.	Husband	149 (42.0)	89 (25.1)	108 (30.4)	199 (56.1)
2.	Wife	66 (18.6)	186 (52.4)	161 (45.4)	49 (13.8)
3.	Jointly	52 (14.7)	20 (5.6)	30 (8.5)	31 (8.7)
4.	Children	52 (14.6)	38 (10.7)	26 (7.3)	34 (9.6)
5.	Others	36 (10.1)	22 (6.2)	30 (8.5)	42 (11.8)
	Total	**355 (100.0)**	**355 (100.0)**	**355 (100.0)**	**355 (100.0)**

Note: Data in Parenthesis is Percentage
Source: Primary Data

This table 5.3 shows that husband motivates greater as regards Television (42 per cent) and Two Wheeler (56 per cent) and his motivation is moderate for Refrigerator (25 per cent) and Washing Machine (30 per cent) while wife dominates as a motivator for Refrigerator (52 per cent) and Washing Machine (45 per cent). Joint motivating role and children's motivating power are not considerable for the purchase decision of selected durables.

Nurturer

Table. 5.4 : Role Structure as Nurturers

Sl. No.	Nurturer	Television	Refrigerator	Washing Machine	Two Wheeler
1.	Husband	206 (58.0)	110 (31.0)	109 (30.7)	192 (54.1)
2.	Wife	47 (13.2)	157 (44.2)	181 (51.0)	58 (16.3)
3.	Jointly	18 (5.1)	19 (5.3)	25 (7.0)	13 (3.7)
4.	Children	76 (21.4)	57 (16.1)	30 (8.5)	74 (20.8)
5.	Others	8 (2.3)	12 (3.4)	10 (2.8)	18 (5.1)
	Total	**355) (100.0**	**355 (100.0)**	**355 (100.0)**	**355 (100.0)**

Note: Data in Parenthesis is Percentage
Source: Primary Data

It can be understood from the table 5.4 that husband is the main nurturer for Television (58 per cent) and Two Wheeler (54 per cent). Similarly, children play a vital role as nurturers for Television (22 per cent), Refrigerator (16 per cent) and for Two Wheeler (21 per cent). Women act as nurturers for Refrigerator (44 per cent) and Washing Machine (51 per cent) whereas the husband's role for Refrigerator and Washing Machine is only 31 per cent.

Time of Purchase

The time of purchase of durables is another important decision to be made. A family can decide to purchase durables during festival time or non-seasonal time or at the time of discount or when they have excess money or when it is urgently needed.

Table 5.5 : Decider of Time of Purchase

Sl. No.	Time Decider	Television	Refrigerator	Washing Machine	Two Wheeler
1.	Husband	211 (59.4)	128 (36.1)	131 (36.9)	259 (73.0)
2.	Wife	60 (16.9)	117 (33.0)	138 (38.8)	42 (11.8)
3.	Jointly	78 (22.0)	98 (27.5)	73 (20.6	32 (9.0)
4.	Children	2 (0.6)	4 (1.1)	11 (3.1)	18 (5.1)
5.	Others	4 (1.1)	8 (2.3)	2 (0.6)	4 (1.1)
	Total	**355 (100.0)**	**355 (100.0)**	**355 (100.0)**	**355 (100.0)**

Note: Data in Parenthesis is Percentage
Source: Primary Data

From the table 5.5 it can be inferred that husband is dominant in deciding the time of purchase of Television (59 per cent), Refrigerator (36 per cent) and Two Wheeler (73 per cent). Women's autonomy regarding time of purchase for Washing Machine is 39 per cent which is more than that of husbands (37 per cent). Here joint decision by husband and wife plays a medium role for Television (21 per cent), Refrigerator (28 per cent), and Washing Machine (21 per cent). Children and others play a less significant role in deciding the time of purchase of selected durables.

Place of Purchase

The place of purchase is another important decision to be taken for family purchase. There will be different stores from which they have to select one and thus decide the place of purchase.

Table 5.6 : Decider of Place of Purchase

Sl. No.	Place Decider	Television	Refrigerator	Washing Machine	Two Wheeler
1.	Husband	241 (67.8)	171 (48.2)	150 (42.3)	246 (69.3)
2.	Wife	50 (14.1)	107 (30.1)	119 (33.5)	26 (7.3)
3.	Jointly	45 (12.7)	39 (11.0)	43 (12.1)	15 (4.2)
4.	Children	8 (2.3)	21 (5.9)	34 (9.6)	22 (6.2)
5.	Others	11 (3.1)	17 (4.8)	9 (2.5)	46 (13.0)
	Total	**355 (100.0)**	**355 (100.0)**	**355 (100.0)**	**355 (100.0)**

Note: Data in Parenthesis is Percentage
Source: Primary Data

This table 5.6 shows that husband is the sole decider for all the selected durables in this regard. His role as a decider for the place of purchase for Television is 68 per cent; Refrigerator is 48 per cent; Washing Machine is 42 per cent and Two Wheeler is 69 per cent. Women are moderate in suggesting the place of purchase for Refrigerator (30 per cent) and Washing Machine (34 per cent) and as regards Television and Two Wheeler, she plays only an insignificant role. Children and others' role is minimal.

Brand of Purchase

The marketer is keen on to note that the decider for a brand is in order to target the person. There are different brands available in the markets which are manufactured by Multi National as well as by Indian Companies.

It can be inferred from the table 5.7 that husband is the decider of the brand for Television (48 per cent) and Two Wheeler (58 per cent). Women's autonomy in choosing the brand for Refrigerator is 49 per cent and Washing Machine is 40 per cent. For these two durables husband's role is average. In the case of Television, joint decision making of the brand is at a medium level (21 per cent). Children have little influence for deciding the brand of Refrigerator, Washing Machine and Two Wheeler. Friends and relatives do have a say as regards deciding the brand of a Two Wheeler (16 per cent).

Table 5.7 : Decider of The Brand

Sl. No.	Brand Decider	Television	Refrigerator	Washing Machine	Two Wheeler
1.	Husband	171 (48.2)	83 (23.4)	118 (33.2)	204 (57.4)
2.	Wife	68 (19.2)	173 (48.7)	143 (40.3)	39 (11.0)
3.	Jointly	75 (21.1)	37 (10.4)	41 (11.6)	18 (5.1)
4.	Children	21 (5.9)	39 (11.0)	36 (10.1)	39 (11.0)
5.	Others	20 (5.6)	23 (6.5)	17 (4.8)	55 (15.5)
	Total	**355 (100.0)**	**355 (100.0)**	**355 (100.0)**	**355 (100.0)**

Note: Data in Parenthesis is Percentage
Source: Primary Data

Colour of Durables

Another important decision to be taken about the purchase of durables is the colour of the durables especially for the purchase of Refrigerator and Two Wheeler. The table 5.8 given below shows the colour deciders of the selected durables.

This table 5.8 shows the colour deciders for the selected durables. Husband dominates in deciding the colour for Television (46 per cent) and Two Wheeler (52 per cent). As regards the colour of Refrigerator (58 per cent) and Washing Machine (58 per cent) the wife is the main decision maker. Children play a considerable role in deciding the colour of Refrigerator (11 per cent) and Two Wheeler (11.3 per cent) and the joint decision regarding colour is just 12 per cent.

Table 5.8 : Colour Deciders

Sl. No.	Colour Decider	Television	Refrigerator	Washing Machine	Two Wheeler
1.	Husband	162 (45.6)	49 (13.8)	63 (17.7)	184 (51.8)
2.	Wife	99 (27.9)	205 (57.7)	204 (57.5)	59 (16.6)
3.	Jointly	45 (12.7)	43 (12.1)	49 (13.8)	29 (8.2)
4.	Children	32 (9.0)	39 (11.0)	28 (7.9)	40 (11.3)
5.	Others	17 (4.8)	19 (5.4)	11 (3.1)	43 (12.1)
	Total	**355 (100.0)**	**355 (100.0)**	**355 (100.0)**	**355 (100.0)**

Note: Data in Parenthesis is Percentage

Source: Primary Data

Model of Durables

Model of the durables is another vital decision to be made before making the purchase. Modernisation has an impact in the introduction of several new models in order to attract customers. It is the prime policy of every manufacturer.

Table 5.9 : Model Deciders

Sl. No.	Model Decider	Television	Refrigerator	Washing Machine	Two Wheeler
1.	Husband	173 (48.7)	90 (25.3)	78 (22.0)	215 (60.6)
2.	Wife	86 (24.2)	186 (52.4)	192 (54.1)	51 (14.4)
3.	Jointly	62 (17.5)	47 (13.2)	42 (11.8)	21 (5.9)
4.	Children	21 (5.9)	13 (3.7)	24 (6.8)	30 (8.4)
5.	Others	13 (3.7)	19 (5.4)	19 (5.3)	38 (10.7)
	Total	**355 (100.0)**	**355 (100.0)**	**355 (100.0)**	**355 (100.0)**

Note: Data in Parenthesis is Percentage

Source: Primary Data

From this table 5.9 it is clear that husband dominates in deciding the model for Television (49 per cent) and Two Wheeler (61 per cent). Wife dominates in deciding the model for Refrigerator (52 per cent) and Washing Machine (54 per cent) where the husband has only a medium role. Joint decision is nominal for deciding the model for Television (18 per cent), Refrigerator (13 per cent) and Washing Machine (12 per cent). Children and non-family members' influence on choosing the model is not significant except for Two Wheelers in which 11 per cent are influenced by others.

Size of the Durables

In order to attract customers from all walks of life, durables are produced in different sizes and marketed. Who decides the size of the selected durables is a vital question to be answered. The table given below shows the decider of the size of the selected durables.

Table 5.10 : Deciders of the Size of Durables

Sl. No.	Size Decider	Television	Refrigerator	Washing Machine	Two Wheeler
1.	Husband	174 (49.0)	106 (29.9)	72 (20.3)	230 (64.8)
2.	Wife	72 (20.3)	190 (53.5)	198 (55.8)	25 (7.0)
3.	Jointly	68 (19.2)	40 (11.3)	45 (12.7)	30 (8.5)
4.	Children	30 (8.4)	7 (2.0)	34 (9.6)	38 (10.7)
5.	Others	11 (3.1)	12 (3.4)	6 (1.7)	32 (9.0)
	Total	**355 (100.0)**	**355 (100.0)**	**355 (100.0)**	**355 (100.0)**

Note: Data in Parenthesis is Percentage
Source: Primary Data

It is clear that for Television and Two Wheeler husband's involvement is greater than others. As regards Refrigerator and washing machine, as wife is more attached to these products, she mostly decides the size of Refrigerator (53 per cent) and Washing Machine (56 per cent). Joint decision by husband and wife is also considerable for Television, Refrigerator and Washing Machine. Husband's involvement for Refrigerator is 30 per cent and Washing Machine is 20 per cent. Others involvement is minimal.

Mode of Purchase

Durables can be purchased on cash down basis or credit basis. What mode should be applied to purchase durables is another important decision to be taken in the purchase of durable goods by family.

Table 5.11 : Mode of Purchase Deciders

Sl. No.	Made Decider	Television	Refrigerator	Washing Machine	Two Wheeler
1.	Husband	234 (65.9)	167 (47.0)	138 (38.9)	237 (66.8)
2.	Wife	17 (4.8)	71 (20.0)	72 (20.3)	23 (6.5)
3.	Jointly	103 (29.0)	108 (30.4)	115 (32.4)	82 (23.1)
4.	Children	0 (0.0)	3 (0.8)	26 (7.3)	10 (2.8)
5.	Others	1 (0.3)	6 (1.7)	4 (1.1)	3 (0.8)
	Total	**355 (100.0)**	**355 (100.0)**	**355 (100.0)**	**355 (100.0)**

Note: Data in Parenthesis is Percentage
Source: Primary Data

It can be inferred from the table 5.11 that husband is the decider regarding the mode of purchase for all the selected durables—for Television (66 per cent), Refrigerator (47 per cent), Washing Machine (39 per cent) and Two Wheeler (67 per cent). Joint decision also plays a role for all the selected durables. Women play a little role in deciding the mode of purchase for Refrigerator (20 per cent) and Washing Machine (20 per cent). The role of children and others is minimal.

Purchaser of a Product

This is an important role to be considered as the final purchase decision making is done by the purchaser who is influenced by the dealers and sales people at the point of purchase.

Table 5.12 : Purchaser of Selected Durables

Sl. No.	Purchaser	Television	Refrigerator	Washing Machine	Two Wheeler
1.	Husband	239 (67.3)	185 (52.1)	159 (44.8)	255 (75.5)
2.	Wife	3 (0.8)	9 (2.5)	18 (5.2)	5 (1.4)
3.	Jointly	77 (21.7)	142 (40.0)	152 (42.6)	48 (13.5)
4.	Children	1 (0.3)	0 (0.0)	19 (5.4)	10 (2.8)
5.	Others	35 (9.9)	19 (5.4)	7 (2.0)	37 (10.4)
	Total	**355 (100.0)**	**355 (100.0)**	**355 (100.0)**	**355 (100.0)**

Note: Data in Parenthesis is Percentage
Source: Primary Data

It is clear from the table 5.12 presented above that husband is the main purchaser for all the products selected for the study. His role as a purchaser for Television is 67 per cent, Refrigerator 52 per cent, Washing Machine 45 per cent and Two Wheeler 76 per cent. Joint purchase is mostly done for women related products like Refrigerator (40 per cent) and Washing Machine (43 per cent). Independent role of women is minimal. Similarly, children and others' role as a purchaser is not significant at all.

Replacement Initiator

Replacement initiator is a person who initiates the replacement of the durables. Marketers are interested in knowing who the replacement initiator is in order to communicate and create the need for replacing the old product for a new one.

Table 5.13 : Replacement Initiator

Sl. No.	Replacement Initiator	Television	Refrigerator	Washing Machine	Two Wheeler
1.	Husband	236 (66.5)	72 (20.3)	65 (18.3)	270 (76.1)
2.	Wife	51 (14.4)	261 (73.5)	237 (66.8)	11 (3.1)
3.	Jointly	24 (6.8)	10 (2.8)	21 (5.9)	12 (3.4)
4.	Children	36 (10.1)	7 (2.0)	30 (8.5)	60 (16.9)
5.	Others	8 (2.3)	5 (1.4)	2 (0.6)	2 (0.6)
	Total	**355 (100.0)**	**355 (100.0)**	**355 (100.0)**	**355 (100.0)**

Note: Data in Parenthesis is Percentage
Source: Primary Data

It is clear from the table shown above that husband dominates in the replacement initiation of Television (67 per cent) and Two Wheeler (76 per cent) while for Refrigerator (74 per cent) and Washing Machine (69 per cent) wife initiates the replacement. Children's influence is moderate for Television (10 per cent) and Two Wheeler (17 per cent).

Role of Women in Family Purchase Decision of Selected Durable Goods

The following table shows the role of women in the family purchase decision of selected durable goods.

From table 5.14 it is clear that women play an insignificant role for the purchase of Television and Two Wheeler. As regards women related products of Refrigerator and Washing Machine, women is dominant in every role except in deciding the time of purchase, the place of purchase, the mode of purchase. Thus it can be concluded that women play a dominant expressive role as regards women related products like Refrigerator and Washing Machine and husband an instrumental role as a purchaser. Regarding Television and Two Wheeler the husband dominates in all these roles.

Table 5.14 : Role of Women in Family Decision Making

Sl. No.	Role	Television	Refrigerator	Washing Machine	Two Wheeler
1.	Initiator	34 (9.5)	196 (55.2)	201 (56.6)	23 (6.5)
2.	Influencer	79 (22.5)	133 (37.5)	159 (44.8)	47 (13.2)
3.	Motivator	66 (18.6)	186 (52.4)	161 (45.4)	49 (13.8)
4.	Nurturer	47 (13.2)	157 (44.2)	181 (51.0)	58 (16.3)
5.	Time deciding	60 (16.9)	117 (33.0)	138 (38.9)	42 (11.8)
6.	Place deciding	50 (14.1)	107 (30.1)	119 (33.9)	26 (7.3)
7.	Brand deciding	68 (19.2)	173 (48.7)	143 (40.3)	39 (11.0)
8.	Colour deciding	99 (27.9)	205 (57.7)	204 (57.5)	59 (16.6)
9.	Model deciding	86 (24.2)	186 (52.4)	192 (54.1)	51 (14.4)
10.	Size deciding	72 (20.3)	190 (53.5)	198 (55.8)	25 (7.0)
11.	Mode of purchase	17 (4.8)	71 (20.0)	72 (20.3)	23 (6.5)
12.	Purchaser	3 (0.8)	9 (2.5)	18 (5.2)	5 (1.4)
13.	Replacement initiator	51 (14.4)	261 (73.5)	237 (66.8)	11 (3.1)

Note: Data in Parenthesis is Percentage

Source: Primary Data

COMPARATIVE STUDY

Relationship between Urban and Rural Families and the Role of Family Purchase Decisions

This part explains the relationship between urban and rural families against the role of members in family purchase decisions.

For the purpose of analysis, chi-square test is used to verify differences in the two areas of residence (urban or rural) with respect to various roles of family decision making such as initiators, influencers, deciders of time, place, brand and, in general, as purchasers.

Initiators

To examine the role dominance as initiators in purchasing durable goods, the respondents were asked as to who in the family would initiate the purchase of selected durables in the two areas of residence. The results are presented in the following table.

Table 5.15 : Role Structure as Initiators

Sl. No.	Product Purchase Decisions	Urban				Rural			
		Television	Refrigerator	Washing Machine	Two Wheeler	Television	Refrigerator	Washing Machine	Two Wheeler
1.	Husband	118 (52.2)	53 (23.5)	36 (15.9)	161 (71.2)	69 (53.5)	36 (27.9)	28 (21.7)	93 (72.1)
2.	Wife	25 (11.1)	123 (54.4)	121 (53.5)	15 (6.6)	9 (7.0)	73 (56.6)	80 (62.0)	8 (6.2)
3.	Children	35 (15.5)	2 (0.8)	5 (2.2)	18 (8.0)	26 (20.2)	1 (0.8)	1 (0.8)	20 (15.5)
4.	Husband & Wife	45 (19.9)	43 (19.0)	50 (22.1)	28 (12.4)	23 (17.8)	14 (10.8)	10 (7.8)	3 (2.3)
5.	Others	3 (1.3)	5 (2.2)	14 (6.2)	4 (1.8)	2 (1.6)	5 (3.9)	10 (7.8)	5 (3.9)
	Total	**226**	**226**	**226**	**226**	**129**	**129**	**129**	**129**

Note: Data in Parenthesis is Percentage
Source: Primary Data

This table 5.15 illustrates that for initiating the purchase of Television and Two Wheeler, husband dominates both in urban and rural families and wife dominates for Refrigerator and Washing Machine in both areas of residence. Children's role for Television and Two Wheeler is little higher in rural families than in urban families. But in contrast, joint initiation role is higher for all the durable goods in urban families than in rural families. Likewise, husband's initiating role is a little higher for all the durable goods in rural area.

Influencers

The influencer's role of family members in urban and rural families is given in the following table 5.16.

This table exhibits clearly the influencers in family purchase decisions between the urban and the rural families. In rural families husband dominates as an influencer for all the selected durable goods, but in urban families he dominates only for Television (55 per cent) and Two Wheeler (65 per cent). For Refrigerator (39 per cent) and Washing Machine (47 per cent) women have more autonomy for gathering information in urban families. For Television and Two Wheeler the rural husband's role as influencer is a little lower than that of the urban husband. The couple acting as influencers is more in rural families than in urban families.

Table 5.16 : Role Structure as Influencers

Sl. No.	Product Purchase Decisions	Urban				Rural			
		Televi-sion	Refrige-rator	Washing Machine	Two Whee-ler	Televi-vision	Refrige-rator	Washing Machine	Two Whee-ler
1.	Husband	125 (55.3)	80 (35.4)	63 (27.9)	148 (64.5)	65 (50.4)	49 (38.0)	55 (42.6)	75 (58.1)
2.	Wife	43 (19.0)	87 (38.5)	106 (46.9)	27 (11.9)	36 (27.9)	46 (35.7)	53 (41.1)	20 (15.5)
3.	Children	26 (11.5)	14 (6.2)	15 (6.6)	25 (11.1)	9 (7.0)	12 (9.3)	5 (3.9)	18 (14.0)
4.	Husband & Wife	17 (7.5)	17 (7.5)	19 (8.4)	17 (7.5)	12 (9.3)	11 (8.5)	6 (4.7)	13 (10.1)
5.	Others	15 (6.6)	28 (12.4)	23 (10.2)	9 (4.0)	7 (5.4)	11 (8.5)	10 (7.8)	1 (2.3)
	Total	**226**	**226**	**226**	**226**	**129**	**129**	**129**	**129**

Note: Data in Parenthesis is Percentage
Source: Primary Data

Time of Purchase

The respondents were asked about 'who' in the family decides the time of purchase of durable goods. The table 5.17 shows the responses of wives regarding the role of family members in deciding about the time of purchase.

The table 5.17 shows that for the purchase of all the four durable goods, the time dimension is usually dominated by husband in urban families. Wives role is also significant for Refrigerator (29 per cent) and washing machine (38 per cent). Joint decision is also made for Television (21 per cent), Refrigerator (28 per cent) and Washing Machine (20 per cent). Children and others do not have any say at all in deciding about the time of purchase of durable goods. In rural families, husband dominates regarding the time of purchase for Television (61 per cent) and Two Wheeler (58 per cent) and wife has an autonomy over Refrigerator (40 per cent) and Washing Machine (40 per cent). Joint decision is average for Television (23 per cent), Refrigerator (27 per cent) and Washing Machine (21 per cent). For Refrigerator (29 per cent) and Washing Machine (35 per cent), husband too contributes to the time of purchase decision. Here too children's and others' role is minimal.

Table 5.17 : Role Structure in Time of Purchase Decisions

Sl. No.	Product Purchase Decisions	Urban				Rural			
		Television	Refrigerator	Washing Machine	Two Wheeler	Television	Refrigerator	Washing Machine	Two Wheeler
1.	Husband	133 (58.8)	91 (40.3)	86 (38.1)	184 (81.4)	78 (60.5)	37 (28.7)	45 (34.9)	75 (58.2)
2.	Wife	43 (19.0)	66 (29.2)	86 (38.1)	14 (6.2)	17 (13.2)	51 (39.5)	52 (40.3)	28 (21.7)
3.	Children	0 (0)	1 (0.4)	7 (3.1)	9 (4.0)	2 (1.6)	3 (2.3)	4 (3.1)	9 (7.0)
4.	Husband & Wife	48 (21.2)	63 (27.9)	46 (20.4)	19 (8.4)	30 (23.2)	35 (27.1)	27 (20.9)	13 (10.0)
5.	Others	2 (0.8)	5 (2.2)	1 (0.4)	0 (0)	2 (1.6)	3 (2.3)	1 (0.8)	4 (3.1)
	Total	**226**	**226**	**226**	**226**	**129**	**129**	**129**	**129**

Note: Data in Parenthesis is Percentage
Source: Primary Data

Place of Purchase

The views of the respondents as regards making the decision in the selection of stores are shown in the form of frequency distribution in the table 5.18.

From this table 5.18 it can be inferred that husband dominates in choosing the store for the purchase of all the durables under study, both in the urban and rural families. Wife has a say as a decider of the place of purchase only for Refrigerator and Washing Machine in both the areas of residence. In 10 per cent of families joint decision is taken for the choice of store of purchase. In rural families, children's views are considered in deciding the store selection for the purchase of Refrigerator (12 per cent) and Washing Machine (15 per cent). So also in urban families, the views of relatives and friends (11 per cent) are taken into account while deciding the place of purchase of Two Wheeler.

Table 5.18 : Role Structure in Place Decision

Sl. No.	Product Purchase Decisions	Urban				Rural			
		Televi-sion	Refrige-rator	Washing Machine	Two Whee-ler	Televi-vision	Refrige-rator	Washing Machine	Two Whee-ler
1.	Husband	154 (68.1)	119 (52.7)	98 (43.4)	162 (71.7)	87 (67.4)	52 (40.3)	52 (40.3)	84 (65.1)
2.	Wife	35 (15.5)	65 (28.8)	78 (34.5)	19 (8.4)	15 (11.6)	42 (32.6)	41 (31.8)	7 (5.4)
3.	Children	6 (2.7)	6 (2.7)	15 (6.6)	11 (4.9)	2 (1.6)	15 (11.6)	19 (14.7)	11 (8.5)
4.	Husband & Wife	23 (10.2)	24 (10.6)	29 (12.8)	10 (4.4)	22 (17.1)	15 (11.6)	14 (10.8)	5 (3.9)
5.	Others	8 (3.5)	12 (5.3)	6 (2.7)	24 (10.6)	3 (2.3)	5 (3.9)	3 (2.3)	22 (4.5)
	Total	**226**	**226**	**226**	**226**	**129**	**129**	**129**	**129**

Note: Data in Parenthesis is Percentage
Source: Primary Data

Brand Decision

To examine the role dominance as regards brand decision of the durables, the respondents were asked as to who in the family decides the brand decision and the result is given in Table 5.19.

The table 5.19 shows that both in urban and rural families the brand decision is mostly taken by husband in the case of Television and Two Wheeler and wife dominates in taking brand decision for Refrigerator and Washing Machine. But interestingly, the children of rural families have more influence in deciding the brand for Refrigerator (14 per cent), Washing Machine (17 per cent) and Two Wheeler (16 per cent) than children in urban families. Joint decision is also significant for Television in both urban (20 per cent) and rural (24 per cent) families. Relatives and friends play an ordinary and equal role in deciding the brand for Two Wheeler (15.5 per cent) both in urban and rural areas.

Table 5.19 : Role Structure in Brand Decision

Sl. No.	Product Purchase Decisions	Urban				Rural			
		Television	Refrigerator	Washing Machine	Two Wheeler	Television	Refrigerator	Washing Machine	Two Wheeler
1.	Husband	104 (46.0)	57 (25.2)	85 (37.6)	141 (62.4)	67 (51.9)	26 (20.2)	33 (25.6)	63 (48.8)
2.	Wife	50 (22.1)	110 (48.7)	93 (41.2)	20 (8.8)	18 (13.9)	63 (48.8)	50 (38.8)	19 (14.7)
3.	Children	18 (8.0)	21 (9.3)	14 (6.2)	18 (8.0)	3 (2.3)	18 (13.9)	22 (17.1)	21 (16.3)
4.	Husband & Wife	44 (19.5)	22 (9.7)	23 (10.2)	12 (5.3)	31 (24.0)	15 (11.6)	18 (13.9)	6 (4.7)
5.	Others	10 (4.4)	16 (7.1)	11 (4.9)	35 (15.5)	10 (7.9)	7 (5.4)	6 (4.7)	20 (15.5)
	Total	**226**	**226**	**226**	**226**	**129**	**129**	**129**	**129**

Note: Data in Parenthesis is Percentage
Source: Primary Data

Purchaser of Durable Goods

To ascertain the role dominance of family members as a purchaser, the responses of wives are given in the following table 5.20 for both urban and rural families.

An analysis of responses as presented in the table 5.20 shows that husband dominates as the purchaser for all durables in both urban and rural families except in the case of Washing Machine in urban families where it is done by the couple jointly. Regarding women related products of Refrigerator and Washing Machine the purchases are done jointly by husband and wife and this is greater in urban families (44 per cent) than in rural families (34 per cent and 32 per cent). For Two Wheeler the husband dominates as a purchaser. Others acting as purchasers are minimal for Two Wheeler (11 per cent) in urban families.

Table 5.20 : Role Structure as Purchasers

Sl. No.	Product Purchase Decisions	Urban				Rural			
		Television	Refrigerator	Washing Machine	Two Wheeler	Television	Refrigerator	Washing Machine	Two Wheeler
1.	Husband	158 (69.9)	112 (49.6)	92 (40.7)	161 (71.2)	81 (62.8)	73 (56.6)	65 (50.4)	94 (72.9)
2.	Wife	2 (0.9)	2 (0.9)	8 (3.5)	3 (1.3)	1 (0.8)	7 (5.4)	12 (9.3)	2 (1.6)
3.	Children	0 (0)	0 (0)	24 (10.6)	3 (1.3)	1 (0.8)	0 (0)	6 (4.7)	7 (5.4)
4.	Husband & Wife	49 (21.7)	98 (43.4)	100 (44.2)	34 (15.0)	28 (21.7)	44 (34.1)	41 (31.8)	14 (10.9)
5.	Others	17 (7.5)	14 (6.2)	2 (0.9)	25 (11.1)	18 (13.9)	5 (3.9)	5 (3.9)	12 (9.3)
	Total	**226**	**226**	**226**	**226**	**129**	**129**	**129**	**129**

Note: Data in Parenthesis is Percentage
Source: Primary Data

Test of Significance

Chi-square test is conducted to test the significant association between urban and rural families with regard to the six roles in family purchase decisions and the result is shown in the following table.

Ho_1: ***There is no significant difference between urban and rural families with regard to role structure in family purchase decision.***

Table 5.21 : Chi-square Test Results

Sl. No.	Role	df	Television	Refrigerator	Washing Wheeler	Two Machine
1.	Initiators	4	2.713	4.956	16.649*	11.691**
2.	Influencers	4	5.503	2.631	18.856*	9.377
3.	Time decision	4	5.677	8.321	0.506	31.513*
4.	Place decision	4	4.774	14.597*	6.279	5.965
5.	Brand decision	4	10.297**	3.155	14.264*	10.447**
6.	Purchasers	4	5.828	10.043**	16.981*	6.269

Note: *Denotes significant at .01 level (Table Value 13.277)
**Denotes significant at .05 level (Table Value 9.488)

From this table 5.21 it can be inferred that there is a significant relationship at one per cent between the initiating role of Washing Machine, influencing role of Washing Machine, time decision of Two Wheeler, place decision of Refrigerator, brand decision of Washing Machine and the role as purchaser for Washing Machine and the urban and rural families.

There is a similar association between urban and rural families and the initiating role of Two Wheeler, brand decision of Television and Two Wheeler and the role as purchaser for Refrigerator at 95 per cent confidence level.

Other roles have no relationship with the rural and urban families at 5 per cent significance level as the calculated value is less than the table value (9.49) and the null hypothesis is accepted.

Comparative Study between Working Women and Non-working Women and the Role of Family Members in Family Purchase Decisions

Two way table is prepared with respect to six roles in family decision making such as initiators, influencers, time of purchase decision, place of purchase decision, brand decision and purchaser and families who have working and non-working women to make a comparative study between these two variables.

Initiators

To know the role dominance as initiators in purchasing durable goods, the respondents were asked as to who in the family initiates the purchase of selected durables and the result with reference to working and non-working women in the families is presented in the table 5.22.

It is evident from the table that in working women families the wife's initiating power is higher for refrigerators (60 per cent) which is only 49 per cent in non-working women families. But in contrary non-working wives have higher autonomy in initiating the purchase of washing machine (58 per cent) than working women (55 per cent) for that product. Husbands initiating role dominates both in the families for the purchase of television and two wheeler, and their role is little higher for initiating the purchase of refrigerator (32 per cent) and washing machine (19 per cent) in non-working women families. In both families joint initiating power is notable.

Table 5.22 : Role Structure as Initiators

		Working				Non-Working			
Sl. No.	**Product Purchase Decisions**	**Televi-sion**	**Refrige-rator**	**Washing Machine**	**Two Whee-ler**	**Televi-vision**	**Refrige-rator**	**Washing Machine**	**Two Whee-ler**
1.	Husband	103 (52.8)	38 (19.5)	34 (17.4)	148 (75.9)	84 (52.5)	51 (31.9)	30 (18.8)	106 (66.3)
2.	Wife	16 (8.2)	117 (60.0)	108 (55.4)	8 (4.1)	18 (11.3)	79 (49.4)	93 (58.1)	15 (9.4)
3.	Children	31 (15.9)	1 (0.5)	5 (2.6)	15 (7.7)	30 (18.8)	2 (1.3)	1 (0.6)	16 (10.0)
4.	Husband & Wife	43 (22.1)	31 (15.9)	36 (18.5)	18 (9.2)	25 (15.6)	26 (16.3)	24 (15.0)	20 (12.5)
5.	Others	2 (1.0)	8 (4.1)	12 (6.2)	6 (3.1)	3 (1.9)	2 (1.3)	12 (7.5)	3 (1.9)
	Total	**195**	**195**	**195**	**195**	**160**	**160**	**160**	**160**

Note: Data in Parenthesis is Percentage

Source: Primary Data

Influencers

The two way table 5.23 showing the influencers role in working and non-working women families is presented below.

The table 5.23 shows the influencing role of family members for the purchase of selected durables. Regarding the purchase of Washing Machine the working women (48 per cent) are more influencing than non-working women (41 per cent). Husband's influencing power is more in non-working women families for Refrigerator (38 per cent) and Washing Machine (36 per cent) which is 35 per cent in the case of Refrigerator and 31 per cent for Washing Machine in working women families. Similarly, husband's influential power is more for television (59 per cent) and two wheeler (66 per cent) in working women families which is only 48 per cent and 59 per cent in non-working women families. Other's role is minimal.

Table 5.23 : Role Structure as Influencers

Sl. No.	Product Purchase Decisions	Working				Non-Working			
		Television	Refrigerator	Washing Machine	Two Wheeler	Television	Refrigerator	Washing Machine	Two Wheeler
1.	Husband	114 (58.5)	68 (34.9)	60 (30.8)	128 (65.6)	76 (47.5)	61 (38.1)	58 (36.3)	95 (59.4)
2.	Wife	44 (22.6)	71 (36.4)	94 (48.2)	23 (11.8)	35 (21.9)	62 (38.8)	65 (40.6)	24 (15.0)
3.	Children	11 (5.6)	14 (7.2)	9 (4.6)	25 (12.8)	24 (15.0)	12 (7.5)	11 (6.9)	18 (11.3)
4.	Husband & Wife	12 (6.2)	17 (8.7)	15 (7.7)	10 (5.1)	17 (10.6)	11 (6.9)	10 (6.3)	20 (12.5)
5.	Others	14 (7.2)	25 (12.8)	17 (8.7)	9 (4.6)	8 (5.0)	14 (8.8)	16 (10.0)	3 (1.9)
	Total	**195**	**195**	**195**	**195**	**160**	**160**	**160**	**160**

Note: Data in Parenthesis is Percentage
Source: Primary Data

Time of Purchase Decision

The cross table regarding the influencer's role with regard to working and non-working women families is presented here.

Table 5.24 : Role Structure in Time of Purchase Decisions

Sl. No.	Product Purchase Decisions	Working				Non-Working			
		Television	Refrigerator	Washing Machine	Two Wheeler	Television	Refrigerator	Washing Machine	Two Wheeler
1.	Husband	115 (59.0)	67 (34.4)	66 (33.8)	148 (75.9)	96 (60.0)	61 (38.1)	65 (40.6)	111 (69.4)
2.	Wife	32 (16.4)	57 (29.2)	77 (39.5)	16 (8.2)	28 (17.5)	60 (37.5)	61 (38.1)	26 (16.3)
3.	Children	2 (1.0)	2 (1.0)	9 (4.6)	10 (5.1)	0 (0.0)	2 (1.3)	2 (1.3)	8 (5.0)
4.	Husband & Wife	45 (23.1)	62 (31.8)	42 (21.5)	21 (10.8)	33 (20.6)	36 (22.5)	31 (19.4)	11 (6.9)
5.	Others	1 (0.5)	7 (3.6)	1 (0.5)	0 (0.0)	3 (1.9)	1 (0.6)	1 (0.6)	4 (2.5)
	Total	**195**	**195**	**195**	**195**	**160**	**160**	**160**	**160**

Note: Data in Parenthesis is Percentage
Source: Primary Data

It is clear from the table 5.24 that husband dominates in deciding the time of purchase of all the selected goods in non-working women families. But in the case of working women families women's autonomy in deciding the time of purchase is for Washing Machine (40 per cent). The couple deciding the time of purchasing of durable goods is little higher in working women families than in non-working women families. Interestingly, regarding the purchase of Television and Two Wheeler, non-working women deciding the purchase time is little higher than that of working women.

Place of Purchase Decision

The answer to the question of who in the family decides the place of purchasing the durable goods in working and non-working women families is given below.

Table 5.25 : Role Structure in Place Decision

Sl. No.	Product Purchase Decisions	Working				Non-Working			
		Television	Refrigerator	Washing Machine	Two Wheeler	Television	Refrigerator	Washing Machine	Two Wheeler
1.	Husband	130 (66.7)	99 (50.8)	87 (44.6)	140 (71.8)	111 (69.4)	72 (45.0)	63 (39.4)	106 (66.3)
2.	Wife	22 (11.3)	51 (26.2)	68 (34.9)	16 (8.2)	28 (17.5)	56 (35.0)	51 (31.9)	10 (6.3)
3.	Children	6 (3.1)	4 (2.1)	12 (6.2)	11 (5.6)	2 (1.3)	17 (10.6)	22 (13.8)	11 (6.9)
4.	Husband & Wife	31 (15.9)	29 (14.9)	24 (12.3)	7 (3.6)	14 (8.8)	10 (6.3)	19 (11.9)	8 (5.0)
5.	Others	6 (3.1)	12 (6.2)	4 (2.1)	21 (10.8)	5 (3.1)	5 (3.1)	5 (3.1)	25 (15.6)
	Total	**195**	**195**	**195**	**195**	**160**	**160**	**160**	**160**

Note: Data in Parenthesis is Percentage
Source: Primary Data

This table clearly shows that in working women and non-working women families husband is the main decider of the place of purchase of all the selected durable goods. Regarding women's role, interestingly, working women's role of place decision is little higher for Washing Machine (35 per cent) but lower for Refrigerator (26 per cent) in comparison with non-working women role for Washing Machine (32 per cent) and Refrigerator (35 per cent). Joint decision is also higher in working women families than non-working women families.

Brand Decision

The cross table 5.26 showing the role of family members in deciding the brand of purchase of the selected goods both in working women and non-working women families is shown below.

Table 5.26 : Role Structure in Brand Decision

Sl. No.	Product Purchase Decisions	Working				Non-Working			
		Television	Refrigerator	Washing Machine	Two Wheeler	Television	Refrigerator	Washing Machine	Two Wheeler
1.	Husband	96 (49.2)	43 (22.1)	65 (33.3)	122 (62.6)	75 (46.9)	40 (25.0)	53 (33.1)	82 (51.3)
2.	Wife	32 (16.4)	89 (45.6)	78 (40.0)	24 (12.3)	36 (22.5)	84 (52.5)	65 (40.6)	15 (9.4)
3.	Children	12 (6.2)	16 (8.2)	17 (8.7)	14 (7.2)	9 (5.6)	23 (14.4)	19 (11.9)	25 (15.6)
4.	Husband & Wife	48 (24.6)	31 (15.9)	25 (12.8)	7 (3.6)	27 (16.9)	6 (3.8)	16 (10.0)	11 (6.9)
5.	Others	7 (3.6)	16 (8.2)	10 (5.1)	28 (14.4)	13 (8.1)	7 (4.4)	7 (4.4)	27 (16.9)
	Total	**195**	**195**	**195**	**195**	**160**	**160**	**160**	**160**

Note: Data in Parenthesis is Percentage
Source: Primary Data

It is informed from the above table that non-working women have greater power of deciding the brand of purchase for Refrigerator (53 per cent) and Washing Machine (41 per cent) than working women for Refrigerator (46 per cent) and Washing Machine (40 per cent). But in the contrary, husbands of working women dominate in taking brand decision for Television (49 per cent) and Two Wheeler (63 per cent) as against husbands of non-working women for

Television (47 per cent) and Two wheeler (51 per cent). Children's influence on brand is higher in non-working women families for Refrigerator (14 per cent), Washing Machine (12 per cent) and Two Wheeler (16 per cent) than in working women families. But the joint decision role is higher in working women families than non-working women families in the brand decision of television and refrigerator.

Purchaser

The purchasing role of working women as compared with that of non-working women families is shown in the table 5.27.

Table 5.27 : Role Structure as Purchasers

		Working				Non-Working			
Sl. No.	Product Purchase Decisions	Television	Refrigerator	Washing Machine	Two Wheeler	Television	Refrigerator	Washing Machine	Two Wheeler
1.	Husband	137 (70.3)	86 (44.1)	82 (42.1)	146 (74.9)	102 (63.8)	99 (61.9)	75 (46.9)	109 (68.1)
2.	Wife	0 (0.0)	5 (2.6)	10 (5.1)	1 (0.5)	3 (1.9)	4 (2.5)	10 (6.3)	4 (2.5)
3.	Children	0 (0.0)	0 (0.0)	19 (9.7)	4 (2.1)	1 (0.6)	0 (0.0)	11 (6.9)	6 (3.8)
4.	Husband & Wife	44 (22.6)	97 (49.7)	81 (41.5)	25 (12.8)	33 (20.6)	45 (28.1)	60 (37.5)	23 (14.4)
5.	Others	14 (7.2)	7 (3.6)	3 (1.5)	19 (9.7)	21 (13.1)	12 (7.5)	4 (2.5)	18 (11.3)
	Total	**195**	**195**	**195**	**195**	**160**	**160**	**160**	**160**

Note: Data in Parenthesis is Percentage
Source: Primary Data

This table shows clearly that husband generally acts as purchaser for Television, Washing Machine and Two Wheeler in both families of working women and non-working women. In working women families usually joint purchase is made for Refrigerator (50 per cent) which is only 28 per cent in non-working women families. For Television and Washing Machine joint purchase is higher in working women families than non-working women families. Husband acting as a purchaser in Television (70 per cent) and Two Wheeler (75 per cent) is higher in working women families than in non-working women families. Friends and relatives playing the role as purchasers is a little higher in non-working women families compared to working women families.

Test of Significance

Ho$_2$: *There is no significant association between working women and non-working women families concerning the role of members in family purchase decision.*

In order to examine the hypothesis whether there is any significant relationship between the working and non-working women families with regard to the six roles in family decision making, chi-square test is employed. The table 5.28 shows the chi-square values and the level of significance.

Table 5.28 : Chi-square Test Results

Sl. No.	Role	df	Television	Refrigerator	Washing Wheeler	Two Machine
1.	Initiators	4	3.613	10.287**	3.016	6.827
2.	Influencers	4	12.624**	2.101	3.133	9.014
3.	Time decision	4	3.406	8.387	4.568	11.677**
4.	Place decision	4	7.352	21.441*	6.515	3.078
5.	Brand decision	4	7.545	18.654*	1.583	10.582**
6.	Purchasers	4	8.731	18.108* (D.f .3)	2.287	4.271

Note: * Denotes significant at .01 levels (Table Value 13.277)
** Denotes significant at .05 level (Table Value 9.488)

This table clearly shows that there is a remarkable relationship at one per cent between the role of place decision, brand decision and as purchasers of Refrigerator in working and non-working women families. Hence it can be concluded that at 99 per cent confidence level these decisions are influenced by employment of women as the calculated value is greater than the table value (13.3) at 1 per cent significant level.

The initiating role of Refrigerator, the influencing role of Television, time decision of Two Wheeler and brand decision of Two Wheeler have significant relationship with working women and non-working women families at 5 per cent significance level. Hence at 95 per cent confidence level, these variables have relationship with each other as null hypothesis is rejected.

Other roles have no relationship with working women and non-working women families as in these cases the null hypothesis is accepted because the calculated chi-square value is less than the table value (9.49) at 95 per cent confidence level.

Conclusion

The role played by family members in the purchase of selected durables goods is explained clearly in this chapter. To conclude, women play a dominant role in the purchase of Refrigerator and Washing Machine as they are more related to these products than Television and Two Wheeler. But husband really dominates in every role on the purchase of Television and Two Wheeler. Again, husband dominates in deciding the time, mode, and place of purchase of all the selected durable goods. Thus, it is a fact that husband plays a dominating role in the purchase of Television and Two Wheeler in which wife has little voice. Similarly, in the purchase of Refrigerator and Washing Machine husband plays the instrumental role as husband decides the time, place and mode of purchase and 'women' in the family play an expressive role in deciding the colour, model, size and brand of such purchase. The comparative study reveals clearly, that there is definite difference in the role played by family members and area of residence and employment of women which are analysed through chi-square test.

Final Decision Makers in the Family Purchase of Durable Goods

Introduction

Household influence means the degree to which the husband or the wife attempts to dominate household decisions. Each member of the family plays different roles in offering suggestion to purchase the durable goods by highlighting the unique feature perceived on the product. But usually one of the members used to dominate to take final decision regarding the purchase of the durable goods. This is being discussed in this chapter.

This chapter comprises four parts. The first part of this chapter highlights the final decision makers in the family and the reason for the husband's domination, which is analysed by using Likerts Five Point Scaling Technique and Factor Analysis. The second part deals with the women's autonomy while making the purchase decisions in the family, which is analysed by selecting suitable independent variables and a dependent variable and the same is analysed by using ANOVA. The third part contains the Multiple Linear Regression Analysis which is used to explain the women's autonomy in making the purchase decisions. The last part deals with the Multiple Discriminant Analysis that helps to predict the variations in women's final decision-making on purchasing the durable goods.

Purchase Decision Makers in the Family

Purchasing durable goods for the family is made after collecting the various information from the known circle and from the advertisement media. The same is usually discussed among the husband and wife, elderly person in the family. In this chapter, an attempt is made to find out the influencer in purchase decision. For this purpose, a dichotomy test is employed and the same is presented in the following table.

Table 6.1 : Final Decision Makers

Final Decision Makers	No. of Respondents	Percentage
Husband	320	90.14
Wife	35	9.86
Total	355	100.00

Souce: Primary Data

It could be seen from the above table that a good majority (90.14 per cent) of the respondents, who are involved in families final decision-making regarding the purchase of durable goods is highly dominated by male respondents, whereas the remaining 9.86 per cent witnesses that the purchase decision of durable goods are made by female category, especially wife. From the analysis, it is found that (husband) masculine gender always dominates in the purchase decision of durable goods.

Respondents' Opinion against Husbands' Domination in Purchase Decision

The study reveals that majority of the respondents expressed that the purchase decision on durable goods are finally decided by the husbands. Hence, the reasons for husband's dominance in purchase decision is analysed by selecting nine statements with the help of Likerts' Five Point Scaling Technique. The details are furnished in the table 6.2.

From the table 6.2 shown above it can be inferred that as 'Husband's taste for durables is good' they dominate in taking the purchase decision and it scores the maximum and gets first rank. Second opinion given by wives is that 'Husband has good knowledge' about durables which gets the second rank. The third and fourth rank go for the variables "Husbands knows better than wives" and "Husband mobilises money". Wives weakness of 'not working', 'uneducated' and 'dependence' are the other reasons expressed by the wives and the wives disagree that as "their choices will not be good" husbands dominate.

Table 6.2 : The Opinion of Wives For Husband's Dominance in Decision Making

S. No. Factors	Strongly Agree	Agree	No Opinion	Disagree	Strongly Disagree	Final Score	Rank
1. His taste is good	212	104	0	4	0	1484	I
2. He has good knowledge	197	111	10	2	0	1463	II
3. He knows better than me	212	76	29	3	0	1457	III
4. He mobilises money	91	169	30	30	0	1281	IV
5. I am not working	39	77	32	107	65	878	V
6. I am uneducated	19	34	124	141	35	810	VI
7. He is dominant	24	73	28	97	98	793	VII
8. I am dependent	8	68	46	96	102	754	VIII
9. My choice will not be good	4	34	81	125	76	725	IX

Factor Analysis

Factor analysis is a very useful method of reducing the complexity of the data by reducing the number of variables. It is an excellent way in identifying the latent factors by analysing correlation among variables and it explains the variables that influence much to the base or dependent variables.

Bartlett's test of Sphericity and KAISER MEYER OLKIN (KMO) measures of sample adequacy are used to test the appropriateness of the factor model and its results are shown below.

Table 6.3 : KMO and Bartlett's Test

	Values
KMO measure of sampling adequacy	.886
Bartlett's test of Sphericity Approx. Chi square	3000.913
df	36
Sig	.000

Bartlett's test is used to test the null hypothesis that the variables are not correlated. Since the approximate chi-square value is 3000.913 at 36 degrees of freedom which is significant at 1 per cent level, the test leads to the rejection of the null hypothesis.

The value of KMO statistics (.886) is also very high. Thus the factor analysis may be considered as an appropriate technique.

The result of factor analysis by Principal Component Analysis to find out how many factors are to be extracted is given below.

Table No. 6.4 : Principal Component Analysis

Components	Initial Eigen Value			Extraction Sums of Squared Loadings			Rotation Sums of Squared Loadings		
	Total	% of Variance	Cum %	Total	% of Variance	Cum %	Total	% of Variance	Cum %
1.	5.652	62.802	62.802	5.652	62.802	62.802	3.762	41.799	41.799
2.	1.035	11.496	74.298	1.035	11.496	74.298	2.925	32.499	74.298

The last column of the above table shows that 2 factors can be extracted together which account for 74.3 per cent of the total 9 variables. Out of these 9 variables are only 2 variables showing influence after extraction and rotation of Principal Component Analysis.

To assign variables which have a higher loading, the Rotated Component Matrix table is extracted by following Varimax with Kaiser Normalisation and its result is shown in Table 6.5.

Table 6.5 : Rotated Component Matrix Table

S. No.	Variables	Male Supremacy	Female Inferiority
1.	His taste is good	.887	
2.	He mobilizes money	.826	
3.	He knows better than me	.882	
4.	He has good knowledge	.907	
5.	I am not working		.745
6.	I am uneducated		.807
7.	I am dependent		.807
8.	My choice will not be good		.742

From the table given above it can be noticed from the first column that the variables 'His taste is good' (loading .887), 'He mobilises money' (loading .826), 'He knows better than me' (loading .882) and 'He has good knowledge' (loading .907) have high loadings close to 1.00 and it can be inferred that factor 1 is a combination of these four variables and it can be named as *'Male Chauvinism'*.

From the second column it can be noticed that the variables 'I (wife) am not working' (loading .745), 'I am uneducated' (loading .807), 'I am dependent' (loading .807) and 'My choice will not be good' (loading .742) have higher loadings and indicate that factor 2 is a combination of these four variables which is related to women and is named as *'Female Inferiority'*.

Thus two variables are identified after condensing the 9 variables. They are 'male chauvinism' and 'female inferiority' regarding the husband's dominance in decision making of the purchase of durables in the family.

Purchase Decision made by Women

Even though women play an important role for the upliftment of the family according to the survey made, women themselves admit that they have a poor decision-making autonomy in the family as only in 9.86 per cent of the respondents family they take the final decision-making for the purchase of durable goods.

Factors Influencing the Dominance of Women in Family Purchase Decision-Making

Only 10 per cent of the respondents opined that women in the family will generally take the final decision for the purchase of the durable goods. Eleven factors are given in order to give their views about taking purchase decision of their own and Likerts Five Point Scaling Technique is adopted in order to find out which group of women in the family take final decision about the purchase of the durable goods.

Table 6.6 : Type of Women as Decision Maker

Sl. No.	Factors	Score	Rank
1.	I am self confident	156	I
2.	I am independent	140	II
3.	I have good knowledge	138	III
4.	I am educated	136	IV
5.	I have economic freedom	135	V
6.	My choice always be good	132	VI
7.	I am working	125	VII
8.	Have money on own	124	VIII
9.	I am dominant	117	IX
10.	Husband is not here	104	X
11.	Husband has no interest	101	XI

Source: Primary Data

It can be identified that the women who are 'self confident' take final decision of purchasing durables as it scores the highest. Second rank is scored by the factor 'independence' in taking decisions. If the women in the family have 'good knowledge' about the product and if they are 'educated' they have the highest score for taking purchase decision as it scores the third and fourth rank respectively. Similarly, if women have 'economic freedom' in the family they get the scope of taking final purchase decision of durables. Dominance or absence of husband or no interest for husband is the least important factor for a woman to take final purchase decision of durables.

Demographic Factors and Women in Decision Making

In order to analyse and find out which group of women are the final decision makers in the family, a two way table is prepared and ANOVA test is employed to test the hypothesis. Eleven independent variables such as age, education, family income, occupation, religion, class, size of family, number of children, wealth position, type of marriage and type of family are chosen for detailed study especially, the women who are involved in final decision making and the results of these analysis are shown below.

Age and Purchase Decision Made by Women

Age is an important factor in decision making. For the purpose of this study, age has been classified into three categories namely Young (below 30 years), Middle Aged (31-40 years) and Old Aged (above 40 years). The sample consists of 11 (31.4) young respondents, 9 middle aged (25.7) and 15 old aged (42.9) respondents. The distribution of sample respondents according to the age of the women and their role in purchase decisions is shown in the following table.

Table No. 6.7 : Age and Women's Purchase Decision

Sl. No.	Age	No. of Respondents	%	Average	Range		
					Min.	Max	S.D
1.	Young (Below 30 years)	11	31.4	23.5	17.0	28.0	3.7
2.	Middle (31-40 years)	9	25.7	26.7	20.0	31.0	4.7
3.	Old (Above 40 years)	15	42.9	26.9	20.0	31.0	3.2
	Total	**35**	**100.0**				

It could be observed from the table given above that the purchase decision of durable goods made by young women ranges between 17 and 28 with an average of 23.5. The decisions taken by middle aged and old aged women range between 20 and 31 with an average of 26.7 and 26.9 respectively. From the analysis, it can be found that women who have crossed above 40 years age group take purchase decision of durables than below 40 years age group.

With a view to find the degree of association between age of the respondents and women's purchase decision, a two way table is prepared and is given in Table 6.8.

It is highlighted from the table 6.8 that good decisions by women in the purchase of durable goods is the highest (46.2) among the old aged women and the same is the lowest (15.4) among young women. The percentage of mediocre decision is also the highest for women above the age of 40 (53.8) and lowest for middle aged women (15.4). Contrary to this, poor decision makers are young women (55.6) and middle and aged women are of the same percentage (22.2) for poor decision-making.

Table 6.8 : Age And Purchase Decision Made By Women (Two-way Table)

Si. No.	Age	Opinion			Total
		Poor	Mediocre	Good	
1.	Young (Below 30 years)	5 (55.6)	4 (30.8)	2 (15.4)	11
2.	Middle (31-40 years)	2 (22.2)	2 (15.4)	5 (38.5)	9
3.	Old (Above 40 years)	2 (22.2)	7 (53.8)	6 (46.2)	15
	Total	**9**	**13**	**13**	**35**

In order to find the relationship between age and opinion of women decision makers ANOVA is employed and the result of the analysis is shown in the following table.

Table. 6.9 : Age and Family Purchase Decision Taken by Women (ANOVA)

Source	SS	DF	MS	F	S
Between Groups	2.466	2	1.233	1.710	Not Significant
Within Groups	23.077	32	0.721		
Total	**25.543**	**34**			

From the table 6.9 it can be inferred that there is no significant relationship between age and women as a decision maker in the purchase of durable goods as the value of F (1.710) at 2.32 degrees of freedom is less than the table value (3.32).

Education and Purchase Decision Made by Women

Education sharpens the mind and shapes the personality of an individual. It also creates awareness and helps to take right decisions. For the purpose of the study the educational qualification of the respondents has been studied under 4 categories namely Below 12th Standard, Under Graduates,

Post Graduates and Professional. The sample consists of 7 (20 per cent) school level educated respondents, 16 Under Graduates (45.7 per cent), 9 (25.7 per cent) Post Graduates and 3 (8.67 per cent) professional women. The following table 6.10 shows the distribution of sample respondents according to education and purchase decision taken by women.

Table 6.10 : Education Level and Opinion on Family Purchase Decision

Si. No.	Education Level	No. of Respondents	%	Average	Range		
					Min.	Max.	S.D
1.	Below 12th	7	20.0	28.0	24.0	30.0	2.8
2.	Under Graduates	16	45.7	26.9	20.0	31.0	3.5
3.	Post Graduates	9	25.7	22.6	17.0	28.0	4.1
4.	Professional	3	8.6	24.3	21.0	26.0	2.9
	Total	**35**	**100.0**				

Table 6.10 shows that the decision taken by school level educated women range between 24 and 30 with an average of 28. The Under Graduate women's purchase decision ranges between 20 and 31 with an average of 26.9 and that of Post Graduate women ranges between 17 and 28 with an average of 22.6. On the other hand decision makers among professional women range between 21 and 26 with an average of 24.3. From this it is inferred that the maximum level of women decision makers is undergraduate respondents.

With a view to find the degree of association between education and women in family decision making, a two way table is prepared and is given below in Table 6.11.

Table 6.11 : Education Level And Opinion on Family Purchase Decision (Two-way Table)

S. No.	Education Level	Opinion			Total
		Poor	Mediocre	Good	
1.	Below 12th	0	2 (15.4)	5 (38.5)	7
2.	Under Graduates	2 (22.2)	8 (61.5)	6 (46.2)	16
3.	Post Graduates	6 (66.7)	1 (7.7)	2 (15.4)	9
4.	Professional	1 (11.1)	2 (15.4)	0	3
	Total	**9 (100.0)**	**13 (100.0)**	**13 (100.0)**	**35**

It is understood from the table 6.11 that the Under Graduates are the good (46.2 per cent) and mediocre (61.5 per cent) among women decision makers rather than professionals and Post Graduates. Poor women decision makers are post-graduates (66.7 per cent) compared to school level respondents Under Graduates and professionals.

In order to find the relationship between educational qualification of the respondents and power of women in family decision making in the purchase of durable goods, ANOVA test is used and the result is shown in the following table 6.12.

Table 6.12 : Education Level and Opinion on Family Purchase Decision (ANOVA)

Source	SS	DF	MS	F	S
Between Groups	6.667	2	3.334	5.466	Significant at 1% level
Within Groups	19.504	32	0.610		
Total	**26.171**	**34**			

The above table 6.12 clearly shows that at 99 per cent confidence level there is significant relationship between education of women and her role as a deciding authority over her spouse, as the critical value of F for 2 and 32 degrees of freedom at 1 per cent level of significance (5.39) is less than the calculated value of F = 5.466 and the null hypothesis is rejected.

Occupation and Women in Family Decision Making

The respect and regard to a common man is determined based on the occupational status. Occupation is a status-quo throughout the globe. In this study, occupation has been classified into four categories namely employees in private concerns, in government sector, home makers and those who are self employed. The sample consists of 9 (25.7 per cent) employees of both government and private sector and 17 (48.6 per cent) home makers.

It can be seen from the table 6.13 that among employees in the private sector women's decision making power ranges between 17 and 31 with an average of 22.6 and for women employees in the government, decision-making level ranges between 20 and 31 with an average of 26.1 while the decision making power of home makers is the maximum with an average score of 27.3. From this analysis it can be concluded that homemakers have a greater decision-making power than employed women.

Table 6.13 : Occupation and Opinion on Family Purchase Decision

Sl. No.	Occupation Status	No. of Respondents	%	Average	Range Min.	Max.	S.D
1.	In Private Corporation	9	25.7	22.6	17.0	31.0	5.
2.	In Govt. Sector	9	25.7	26.1	20.0	31.0	4.
3.	Home makers	17	48.6	27.3	24.0	30.0	2.
	Total	**35**	**100.0**				

With a view to find the degree of association between occupation and decision making power among women, a two way table is prepared and is presented in Table 6.14.

Table 6.14 : Occupation and Opinion on Family Purchase Decision (Two-way Table)

S. No.	Education Level	Opinion			Total
		Poor	Mediocre	Good	
1.	In Private Corporation	7 (77.8)	0	2 (15.4)	9
2.	In Govt. Sector	2 (22.2)	5 (38.5)	2 (15.4)	9
3.	Home makers	0	8 (61.5)	9 (69.2)	17
	Total	**9**	**13**	**13**	**35**

The table 6.14 shows that good (69.2 per cent) and medium (61.5 per cent) decision-makers are home makers rather than working women while poor women decision makers are the workers of private concern (77.8 per cent) and government employees (22.2 per cent).

To find out the relationship between the occupation and decision-making power of women, Analysis of Variance is used and the result is shown in Table 6.15.

Table 6.15 : Occupation and Opinion on Family Purchase Decision (ANOVA)

Source	SS	DF	MS	F	S
Between Groups	49.233	2	24.616	16.600	Significant at 1% level
Within Groups	47.453	32	1.483		
Total	**96.686**	**34**			

Since the table 6.15 shows that calculated value of F (16.600) is more than the table value at 99 per cent confidence level, the null hypothesis is rejected and so there is a good relationship between occupation and women as a dominant role in decision making in the purchase of durable goods.

Monthly Family Income and Purchase Decision of Women

Income is the major source for a happy life. The earning capacity increases the purchasing power in the family and hence an important factor for family decision making. The family income generated per month is studied under three categories *viz.,* Below Rs. 20000, between Rs. 20001 and 40000 and income above Rs. 40000 per month.

Table 6.16 : Monthly Family Income and Women in Purchase Decison

Sl. No.	Monthly Income	No. of Respondents	%	Average	Range		
					Min.	Max.	S.D
1.	Below Rs. 20000	13	37.1	27.9	21.0	31.0	3.4
2.	Rs.20001-40000	5	14.3	27.6	27.0	30.0	1.3
3.	Above Rs. 40000	17	48.6	23.6	20.0	27.0	3.3
	Total	**35**	**100.0**				

It can be observed from the table 6.16 that the purchase decision taken by women among low income group ranges between 21 and 31 with an average of 27.9. The decision taken by women in middle class income group (Rs. 20001 to

Rs. 40000 per month) ranges between 27 and 30 with an average of 27.6, and high level income group ranges between 20 and 27 and its average is 23.6. Thus it can be inferred that women in low family income group takes final purchase decision of durable goods more than women in other income groups.

To find the degree of association between family income and women's autonomy in family purchase decision, a two way table is prepared which is given in Table 6.17.

Table 6.17 : Monthly Family Income and Women in Decision Making (Two-way Table)

S. No.	Monthly Income	Opinion			Total
		Poor	Mediocre	Good	
1.	Below Rs. 20000	1 (11.1)	4 (30.8)	8 (61.5)	13
2.	Rs. 20001-40000	0	4 (30.8)	1 (7.7)	5
3.	Above Rs. 40000	8 (88.9)	5 (38.5)	4 (30.8)	17
	Total	**9**	**13**	**13**	**35**

It can be inferred from the table 6.17 that good women decision makers are high (61.5) among low income group *i.e.*, the family earning below Rs. 20000 per month and low among medium (7.7) and high income group (30.8). The percentage of mediocre decision is high among high income group (38.5 per cent) rather than low and medium income group of women. Similarly, poor decision makers are among high income group (88.9 per cent) rather than low income group of women. ANOVA has been employed to find the relationship between family income and women decision makers and the result is shown in Table 6.18.

From the table 6.18 it can be inferred that there is no significant association between monthly family income and women in decision-making as the value of F (0.986) at 2,32 degrees of freedom is less than the table value.

Table 6.18 : Monthly Income and Opinion on Family Purchase Decision (ANOVA)

Source	SS	DF	MS	F	S
Between Groups	6.310	2	3.155	0.986	Not Significant
Within Groups	102.376	32	3.199		
Total	**108.686**	**34**			

Religion and Women in Purchase Decision

Religious differences may influence customers in terms of their seasonality of purchases guided by their festival dates, which is a visible manifestation of influence on items of purchase and gifts. For the purpose of this study the respondents are divided into Hindus, Christians and Muslims. The role of women belonging to various religions in decision making is shown in Table 6.19.

Table 6.19 : Religion and Opinion on Family Purchase Decision

Si. No.	Religion	No. of Respondents	%	Average	Range		
					Min.	Max.	S.D
1.	Hindu	10	28.6	25.3	17.0	30.0	4.3
2.	Christian	21	60.0	27.0	27.0	27.0	.0
3.	Muslim	4	11.4	25.8	20.0	31.0	4.2
	Total	**35**	**100.0**				

It is identified from the table 6.19 that the role of Hindu women in decision-making ranges from 17 to 30 with an average of 25.3. While Muslim women play an important role in decision-making with their level ranging between 20 and 31 with an average of 25.8 and Christian women's role in decision-making has the same level with an average of 27. From this it is found that Christian women's role in family decision making is higher than that of Hindu and Muslim women.

A two way table is prepared to find out the degree of association between Religion and women's role in family decision making and is presented in the table 6.20.

Table 6.20 : Religion and Opinion on Family Purchase Decision (Two-way Table)

S. No.	Religion	Opinion			Total
		Poor	Mediocre	Good	
1.	Hindu	2 (22.2)	3 (23.1)	5 (38.5)	10
2.	Christian	7 (77.8)	6 (46.2)	8 (61.5)	21
3.	Muslim	0	4 (30.8)	0	4
	Total	**9**	**13**	**13**	**35**

It can be inferred that women as good decision makers are Christian women as it ranks highest with 61.5 per cent. While the score of Hindu women's role is 38.5 per cent. For mediocre decision influence Christian women have a lead over Muslim women (30.8 per cent) and Hindu women (23.1 per cent) while poor decision makers are also headed by Christian women 77.8 per cent and Hindus (22.2 per cent)

Analysis of Variance (ANOVA) is employed to find the relationship between religion and women's influence in family decision making and the result is shown in the table below.

Table 6.21 : Religion and Opinion on Family Purchase Decision (ANOVA)

Source	SS	DF	MS	F	S
Between Groups	1.416	2	.708	1.960	Not Significant
Within Groups	11.556	32	.361		
Total	**12.971**	**34**			

Since the calculated value of *f* (1.960) at 2, 32 *df* is less than the table value, there is no significant relationship between women as a final decision maker and the religion to which they belong.

Community and Women Decision Makers

Caste and creed play an important role in purchase decision making as its role differs from one community to another.

Every community has its own code of conduct, traditional values and beliefs. For this study, community is divided into Forward Caste (F.C), Backward Caste (B.C) and Scheduled Caste (S.C). Among the women decision makers B.C are leading by 74.3 per cent. While O.C's and S.C's are 20 per cent and 5.7 per cent respectively.

Table 6.22 : Community and Opinion on Family Purchase Decision

Sl. No.	Community	No. of Respondents	%	Average	Range		
					Min.	Max.	S.D
1.	Forward Caste	7	20.0	23.9	17.0	28.0	4.4
2.	Backward Caste	26	74.3	26.3	20.0	31.0	3.9
3.	Scheduled Caste	2	5.7	24.0	24.0	24.0	.0
	Total	**35**	**100.0**				

It can be understood from the table given above that women decision makers of Backward Caste range between 20 and 31 with an average of 26.3 while Forward Caste decision making power among women ranges between 17 and 28 with an average of 23.9 and Scheduled Caste women's role has an equal level to decide with an average of 24. Thus it can be concluded that Backward Caste women plays a good role in family decision making for the purchase of major durable goods compared to other caste women.

To find the degree of association between community and women in decision-making the following two way table is prepared.

Table 6.23 : Community and Opinion on Family Purchase Decision (Two-way Table)

S. No.	Community	Opinion			Total
		Poor	Mediocre	Good	
1.	Forward Caste	2 (22.2)	3 (23.1)	2 (15.4)	7
2.	Backward Caste	7 (77.8)	8 (61.5)	11 (84.6)	26
3.	Scheduled Caste	0	2 (15.4)	0	2
	Total	**9**	**13**	**13**	**35**

It can be understood that Good (84.6 per cent), medium (61.5 per cent) and poor (77.8 per cent) decision-making role among women is led by Backward Caste's over Forward Caste and Scheduled Caste.

ANOVA is employed to find out the relationship between these two variables and its final result is shown below.

Table 6.24 : Community and Opinion on Family Purchase Decision (ANOVA)

Source	SS	DF	MS	F	S
Between Groups	.484	2	.242	.503	Not Significant
Within Groups	15.402	32	.481		
Total	**15.886**	**34**			

The above result shows that for (2,32) *df* the calculated value of *f* (.503) is less than the table value, the null hypothesis is accepted and so there is no significant relationship between community and women in decision-making when compared to men.

Area of Residence

In India, over two thirds of the population lives in the rural areas. Urban India also has a significant migratory population which is rooted in villages. There is a vast diversity of income and there are distinct income categories. The women who take purchase decision consist of 54.3 per cent urban women and 45.7 per cent rural women. The following table shows the distribution of women in purchase decision of durables from the point of residence.

Table 6.25 Location of House and Opinion on Family Purchase Decision

Si. No.	Location	No. of Respondents	%	Average	Range		
					Min.	Max.	S.D
1.	Urban	19	54.3	24.4	17.0	31.0	4.3
2.	Rural	16	45.7	27.4	21.0	31.0	2.8
	Total	**35**	**100.0**				

It could be observed from the table 6.25 the urban women who usually take purchase decision range between 17 and 31 with an average of 24.4 while for the rural women it ranges between 21 and 31 with an average of 27.4. From this it is identified that rural women have a greater influence to take purchase decisions than urban women.

A two-way table is prepared to find the degree of association between area of residence and women in purchase decision and is depicted in Table 6.26.

Table 6.26 : Location of House and Opinion on Family Purchase Decision (Two-way Table)

S. No.	Location	Opinion			Total
		Poor	Mediocre	Good	
1.	Urban	8 (88.9)	5 (38.5)	6 (46.2)	19
2.	Rural	1 (11.1)	8 (61.5)	7 (53.8)	16
	Total	**9**	**13**	**13**	**35**

It can be seen from the table given above that medium 61.5 per cent and good (53.8) decision makers are rural women compared to urban women. Similarly, poor decision makers are urban women (88.9 per cent) who outdo the rural women.

In order to find out the relationship between the location of residence and women in decision-making power ANOVA is applied and the result is shown below.

Table 6.27 : Location of House and Opinion on Family Purchase Decision (ANOVA)

Source	SS	DF	MS	F	S
Between Groups	1.489	2	.745	3.311	Significant at 5% level
Within Groups	7.197	32	.225		
Total	**8.686**	**34**			

The ANOVA result shows that *f* value (3.311) is more than the table value at 5 per cent level of significance. The null hypothesis is rejected. Hence there is significant relationship between the location of residence and women as a decision maker at 95 per cent confidence level.

Family Size and Women in Decision-Making

The size of the family is one of the important variables in family decision making. The family may be a small one (upto 3 members) or medium sized (3-5 members) or big (more than 5 members). The sample consists of 14 (40 per cent) small families, 12 (34.3 per cent) medium sized families and 9 big families where women influence purchase decision. The table given below shows the distribution of sample respondents where women take purchase decision according to the size of the family.

Table 6.28 : Family Size and Opinion on Family Purchase Decision

Sl. No.	Size of Family	No. of Respondents	%	Average	Range		
					Min.	Max.	S.D
1.	Small (Upto 3 members)	14	40.0	24.9	17.0	31.0	4.3
2.	Medium (4-5 members)	12	34.3	25.5	20.0	31.0	4.4
3.	Big (Above 5 members)	9	25.7	27.4	24.0	30.0	2.7
	Total	**35**	**100.0**				

It could be understood from the table shown above that the purchase decision by women is greater in big families (27.4) as the decision level varies between 24 and 30. Next are the medium sized families as the level of women in decision making ranges between 20 and 31 with an average of 25.5. In small families it ranges between 17 and 31 with an average of 24.9 and thus it can be said that women in big families influence greater in decision-making than women in small families.

The table 6.29 is the two way cross table which is prepared in order to find the association between women as decision-makers and the size of the family.

Table 6.29 : Family Size and Opinion on Family Purchase Decision (Two-way Table)

S. No.	Size of Family	Opinion			Total
		Poor	Mediocre	Good	
1.	Small (Upto 3 members)	5 (55.6)	5 (38.5)	4 (30.8)	14
2.	Medium (4-5 members)	4 (44.4)	4 (30.8)	4 (30.8)	12
3.	Big (Above 5 members)	0	4 (30.8)	5 (38.5)	7
	Total	**9**	**13**	**13**	**35**

It can be inferred from the table shown above that women are good decision-makers in big families (38.5 per cent) compared to medium and small sized families (30.8 per cent). Decision-making power is medium in small families (38.5 per cent). Women are poor decision-makers in small families (55 per cent).

Analysis of Variance is applied to find out the association between family size and women in decision making and the result is shown below.

Table 6.30 : Family Size and Opinion on Family Purchase Decision (Anova)

Source	SS	DF	MS	F	S
Between Groups	4.749	2	2.375	2.220	Not Significant
Within Groups	34.222	32	1.069		
Total	**38.971**	**34**			

The above result shows that there is no significant relationship between family size and women in decision-making.

Number of Children and Women's Power in Decision-making

Number of children in the family also is a deciding factor for the purchase of durables and family decision making. This variable is divided into two namely family having one child and family having at least 2 children. The family sample in which women take purchase decision consists of 65.7 of the family having one child and 34.3 of the family having 2 children and more. The distribution of sample respondents according to the number of children and women as a decision maker is shown in the following table.

Table 6.31 : Number of Children and Opinion on Family Purchase Decision

Si. No.	No. of Children	No. of Respondents	%	Average	Range Min.	Max.	S.D
1.	One	12	34.3	24.3	17.0	31.0	4.4
2.	2 and above 2	23	65.7	25.9	20.0	31.0	3.7
	Total	**35**	**100.0**				

It could be seen from the table shown above that women take purchase decision of durables in the family having at least 2 children (25.9) with the range varying between 20 and 31. While in the family having one child, women's role ranges between 17 and 31 with an average of 24.3 and so it can be said that in the family having at least 2 children women play a considerable role in decision-making.

With a view to knowing the degree of association between the number of children and women's decision-making role two way cross table is prepared and is shown below.

Table 6.32 : Number of Children and Opinion on Family Purchase Decision (Two-way Table)

S. No.	No. of Children	Opinion			Total
		Poor	Mediocre	Good	
1.	One	5 (55.6)	5 (38.5)	2 (15.4)	12
2.	2 and above 2	4 (44.4)	8 (61.5)	11 (84.6)	23
	Total	**9**	**13**	**13**	**35**

It could be noted from the table shown above that good and medium women decision makers are in families having 2 children and poor women decision maker is in the family having one child (55.6 per cent).

Analysis of Variance (ANOVA) is used to find out the association between the number of children in the family and women as purchase decision maker and the result is shown below.

Table 6.33 : Number of Children and Opinion on Family Purchase Decision (ANOVA)

Source	SS	DF	MS	F	S
Between Groups	2.674	2	1.337	1.423	Not Significant
Within Groups	30.068	32	.940		
Total	**32.743**	**34**			

The ANOVA result shows that the number of children in the family and women playing a good role as a decision maker are not significant and so there is no relationship between these two variables.

Wealth Position of the Family and Women as a Purchase Decision Maker

Wealth is a status symbol in the society and the individual is respected greater based on his/her wealth position rather than education, religion or age. For the purpose of this study wealth is classified into two, namely wealth below Rs. 20 lakhs and wealth above Rs. 20 lakhs. The sample consists of 17 cases of (48.6 per cent) wealth below 20 lakhs and 18 (51.4 per cent) of wealth above Rs. 20 lakhs. The classification of women as decision maker according to wealth table is shown below.

Table 6.34 : Wealth Position and Opinion on Family Purchase Decision

Sl. No.	Wealth Position	No. of Respondents	%	Average	Range		
					Min.	Max.	S.D
1.	Below Rs. 20,00,000	17	48.6	30.0	30.0	30.0	.0
2.	Above Rs. 20,00,000	18	51.4	25.0	17.0	31.0	4.5
	Total	**35**	**100.0**				

It is seen from the table 6.34 that women having high wealth position below Rs. 20 lakhs uniformly range with an average of 30 while the range of women as decision maker for the wealth position above Rs. 20 lakhs range between 17 and 31 with an average of 25. So it can be concluded that in a medium wealthy family, women play a significant role in decision making. The following two way table shows the degree of association between family's wealth and women as a decision maker.

Table 6.35 : Wealth Position and Opinion on Family Purchase Decision (Two-way Table)

Sl. No.	Wealth Position	Opinion			Total
		Poor	Mediocre	Good	
1.	Below Rs. 20,00,000	4 (44.4)	6 (46.2)	7 (53.8)	14
2.	Above Rs. 20,00,000	5 (55.6)	7 (53.8)	6 (46.2)	18
	Total	**9**	**13**	**13**	**35**

The table 6.35 shows that good decision makers are 53.8 per cent, mediocre are 46.2 per cent and poor 44.4 per cent among women having a wealth below Rs. 20,00,000. Women having a wealth above Rs. 20,00,000 are poor decision makers.

The result of ANOVA test is given below.

Table 6.36 : Wealth Position and Opinion on Family Purchase Decision (ANOVA)

Source	SS	DF	MS	F	S
Between Groups	.859	2	0.430	0.261	Not Significant
Within Groups	52.684	32	1.646		
Total	**53.543**	**34**			

From the result shown in table 6.36 it can be concluded that there is no significant relationship between families' wealth position and women as a decision maker in the family for the purchase of durable goods.

Family Type and Women as Decision-maker

Husband, wife and children living together constitute a nuclear family. The nuclear family with at least one grandparent living within the household is called an extended family. The incidences of the extended family have declined because of the geographic mobility that splits up families. The distribution of sample respondents where women dominate in taking purchase decisions from the point of view of family type is given below.

Table 6.37 : Family Type and Opinion on Family Purchase Decision

Sl. No.	Family Type	No. of Respondents	%	Average	Range		
					Min.	Max.	S.D
1.	Nuclear Family	29	82.9	27.0	24.0	29.0	2.4
2.	Joint Family	6	17.1	25.5	17.0	31.0	4.2
	Total	**35**	**100.0**				

The table given above clearly shows that women's role in decision-making ranges between 17 and 31 with an average of 25.5 in a joint family but in a nuclear family it varies between 24 and 29 with only an average of 27. Thus it can be concluded that women in nuclear families influence more in decision-making than women in a nuclear family. A two way table is prepared to find the degree of association between the family type and women as a dominant figure in decision-making and is shown below.

Table 6.38 : Family Type and Opinion on Family Purchase Decision (Two-way Table)

S. No.	Family Type	Opinion			Total
		Poor	Mediocre	Good	
1.	Nuclear Family	9 (100.0)	11 (84.6)	9 (69.2)	29
2.	Joint Family	0	2 (15.4)	4 (30.8)	6
	Total	**9**	**13**	**13**	**35**

It is seen from the table 6.38 that women in a nuclear family are good (69.2 per cent), mediocre (84.6 per cent) and poor (100 per cent) decision makers for the purchase of durables rather than women in a joint family.

In order to find the relationship between the family type and the role of women as final decision makers in the family, Analysis of Variance is made and the result is shown in Table 6.39.

Table 6.39 : Family Type and Opinion on Family Purchase Decision (ANOVA)

Source	SS	DF	MS	F	S
Between Groups	.510	2	.255	1.829	Not Significant
Within Groups	4.462	32	.139		
Total	4.971	34			

It can be noted from the table 6.39 that calculated *f* value (1.829) is less than the table value at 2, 32 degrees of freedom. There is no significant relationship between the family type and women in decision making.

Multiple Regression Analysis

A Regression is a statistical tool used to explain the variation of one dependent based on the variation in one or more independent variables. If there is only one dependent variable and one independent variable used to explain the variation in it, then the model is known as a simple regression. If multiple independent variables are used to explain the variation in a dependent variable, it is called a Multiple Regression model.

The general Multiple Linear Regression model is of the type

$$y = a + b_1x_1 + b_2x_2 + ... + b_nx_n$$

Where y is the dependent variable and $x_1, x_2, x_3... x_n$ are the independent variables expected to be related to y and expected to explain or predict y. $b_1, b_2, b_3 ... b_n$ are the co-efficient of the respective independent variables.

In this study Multiple Linear Regression Analysis is used to explain the dependent variable of the purchase decision made by women based on the variation of eleven independent variables. Independent variables include demographic and socio-economic factors like wife's age, education, family income, status, religion, community, area, family size, number of children, wealth position and family type.

The regression model is

$$y = a + b_1x_1 + b_2x_2 + \ldots\ldots + b_nx_n$$

Where

y = Purchase decision of durables taken by women

x_1 = Age of women

x_2 = Education of women

x_3 = Occupation of women

x_4 = Monthly family income

x_5 = Religion

x_6 = Community

x_7 = Area of living

x_8 = Family size

x_9 = Number of children

x_{10} = Wealth position

x_{11} = Family type

The result of Multiple Regression Analysis is shown below

Table 6.40 : Multiple Regression Analysis

Sl. No.	Variables	Unstandardised Co-efficients		Standardised coefficients	t	Sig.
		B	Std. Error			
	Constant	1.359	0.837			
1.	Age	–0.023	0.143	–0.023	–0.183	NS
2.	Education Level	0.196	0.141	0.175	1.391	NS
3.	Occupation	0.405	0.087	0.696	4.674	1%
4.	Monthly income	–0.293	0.091	–0.534	–3.216	1%
5.	Religion	0.408	0.202	0.256	2.018	10%
6.	Community	0.111	0.147	0.077	0.752	NS
7.	Area	–1.410	0.294	–0.726	–4.787	1%
8.	Family size	0.534	0.122	0.583	4.385	1%
9.	No. of Children	0.279	0.148	0.023	0.189	NS
10.	Wealth Position	–0.098	0.089	–0.125	–1.107	NS
11.	Family Type	–1.093	0.307	–.426	–3.564	1%

R. value	R^2 value	$D.f\,v_1$	$D.f\,v_2$	*f* value	Significance
0.919	0.844	11	23	11.313	1% level

From the table given above it can be inferred that the R^2 value is 0.844 and t-tests for significance of individual independent variables indicates that at the significance level of 0.01 (equivalent to a confidence level of 99%) occupational status, monthly income, family size and family area of residence type are statistically significant and religion is significant at 90 per cent confidence level. Women's age, education level, community, number of children and family wealth position are not statistically significant in each case. The regression equation inferred is

Purchase decision taken by women (Y)

= 1.36 – .02 (age) + .2 (education) +.41 (occupation) – .29 (monthly income) + .41 (religion) + .11 (community) – 1.41 (area) + .53 (family size) + .03 (no. of children) – .1 (wealth) – 1.1 (family type)

The equation obtained above means that women will take purchase decision if women's education, occupation, community, family size and number of children increase and there is decrease in age, income, area of location and family type.

The multiple regression component (dependent variable) is found statistically a good fit as R^2 value is 0.84. It shows that six independent variables contribute at about 84 per cent on the prediction of women taking decision for the purchase of durable goods. Hence the six variables of occupation, monthly income, religion, area of location, family size and family type are the better predictors for the women's autonomy in family purchase decisions.

Multiple Discriminant Function Analysis (MDFA)

Opinion of women towards family purchase decision varies according to the purchase decision of family members. In the study area out of 35 women respondents divided into two groups, one is poor level of opinion towards their family purchase decision and the other is good opinion towards their family purchase decision. The difference of opinion of the respondents in one group from the other is studied with the help of Multiple Discriminant Function Analysis (MDFA). For the purpose of the study eleven independent variables are selected.

1. Age
2. Education
3. Occupation
4. Income
5. Religion
6. Community
7. Area of residence
8. Family size
9. Number of children
10. Wealth
11. Family type

The Multiple Discriminant Function Analysis attempts to construct a function with these and other variables so that the respondents belonging to these two groups are differentiated at the maximum. The linear combination of variables is known as discriminant function and its parameters are called discriminant function coefficients. In constructing this discriminant function all the variables which contribute more to differentiate these two groups are examined.

Mahalanobis minimum D^2 method is based on the generalised squared Euclidean distance that adjusts for unequal variances in the variables. The major advantage of this procedure is that it is computed in the original space of the predictor (independent) variables rather than as a collapsed version which is used in the other method.

Generally, all the variables selected will not contribute to explain the maximum discriminatory power of the function. So a selection rule is applied based on certain criteria to include those variables which best discriminate. Step-wise selection method is applied in constructing discriminant function which selects one variable at a time to include in the function. Before entering into the function the variables are examined for inclusion in the function.

The variables which could have maximum D^2 value, if entered into the function is selected for inclusion in the function. Once entered any variable already in the equation is again considered for removal based on certain removal criteria. Likewise, at each step the next best discriminating variable is selected and included in the function and any variable already included in the function is considered for removal based on the selection and removal criteria respectively.

Multiple Discriminant Analysis for the Women's Level in Decision Making

Since Multiple Discriminant Function Analysis involved classification problem also to ascertain the efficiency of the Multiple Discriminant Function Analysis all the variables which satisfy the entry and removal criteria were entered into the function. Normally the criteria used to select the variables for inclusion in the function is minimum F to enter into the equation (*i.e.*) F statistic calculated for the qualified variable to enter into the function is fixed as ≥ 1.

Similarly any variable entered in the equation will be removed from the function if F statistic for the variable calculated is <1. The two groups are defined as

Group 1 - Low level decision making

Group 2 - High level decision making

The over all Step-wise MDFA results after all significant discriminators have been included in the estimation of discriminated function is given in the following table 6.41.

Table 6.41 : Summary Table Between Low Level and High Level Groups

Step	Variable entered	Wilk's lambda	Minimum D^2	Significance
1.	Age	0.798	1.620	*
2.	Occupation	0.693	1.742	*
3.	Income	0.603	1.789	*

* Significant at 1 per cent level

The summary table indicates that the variable age entered in step 1, Occupation entered in step 2 and variable Income entered in the step 3. The variables age, occupation and Income are significant at 1 per cent level. All the variables are significant discriminator's based on their Wilk's Lambda and D^2 value. The multivariate aspect of the model is given in the following table.

Table 6.42 : Canonical Discriminant Function (Between Low Level and High Level Groups)

Canonical correlation	Wilks Lambda	Chi-square	D.F.	Sig
0.630	0.603	15.927	3	Significant at 1% level

The canonical correlation is 0.603 when squared is 0.364 that is 36 per cent of the variance in the discriminant group can be accounted for by this model, Wilk's Lambda and chi-square value suggest that D.F. is significant at 1 per cent level.

The variables given above are identified finally by the MDFA as the eligible discriminating variables. Based on the selected variables the corresponding D.F. coefficients are calculated. They are given in the following table.

Table 6.43 : Discriminant Function Coefficients (Between Low Level and High Level Groups)

Age	0.799
Occupation	0.381
Income	-0.651
Constant	-1.630

$Z = -1.630 + 0.799\ (\text{Age}) + 0.381\ (\text{Occupation}) -0.651(\text{Income})$

Using this D.F. coefficients and variables discriminating scores for 2 groups are found out and are called group centroids or group means.

For low level (Z_1) it is – 1.025

For high level (Z_2) it is + 0.605

Discriminating factor is the weighted average of Z_1 and Z_2.

$$(i.e)\ Z = \frac{(13 \times Z_1) + (22 \times Z_2)}{13 + 22}$$

if it is represented diagrammatically it will be

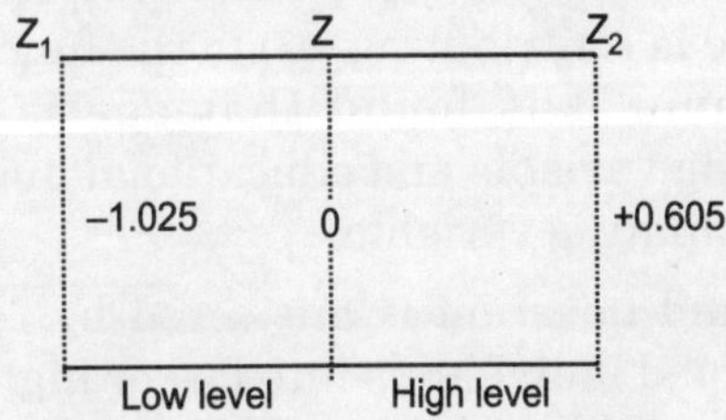

Thus to classify any respondent as to low or high level in decision making the Z score for the respondent is found out by using the equation. If the score found out for any respondent is Z_0 and if the value is $>Z$ (*i.e.* $Z_0 > Z$) then it is classified into high level decision-making and if $Z_0 < Z$ then (*i.e.* $Z_0 < Z$) it is classified in the low level in decision-making

Now the questions remain to be answered are

1. How efficient are the discriminating variables in the MDFA?
2. How efficient the D.F. itself is?

The first question cannot be answered directly however, the discriminating power or the contribution of each variable to the function can sufficiently answer the question. For this consider the following table 6.44.

Table 6.44 : Relative Discriminating Index (Between Low Level and High Level Groups)

	Group 1 Mean X_1	Group 2 Mean X_2	Unstandardised Dic. Coeff. (*kj*)	I_j = ABS (K_j) Mean $(X_{jo} - X_{jl})$	*Rj* = *Ij* / sum *Ij* *j** 100
Age	1.615	2.409	0.799	0.794	27.10
Occupation	2.538	4.000	0.381	1.462	49.90
Income	2.538	1.864	-0.651	0.674	23.00
	Total			**2.930**	**100.00**

Relative Discriminating Index

For each variable the respective D.F. co-efficient, its mean for each group and R_j are given. R_j called relative discriminating index is calculated from the discriminant function coefficient and group means. R_j tells us how much each variable is contributing (%) to the function. By looking at this column it is found that age is the maximum discriminating variable and educational qualification is the least discriminating variable.

The second question is answered by reclassifying the already grouped individuals into low or high level using the D.F.(Z) defined in the equation. This reclassification is called predictor group membership. In short, the efficiency of the D.F. is how correctly it predicts the respondents into respective groups.

Table 6.45 : Classification Results (Between Low Level and High Level Group)

Actual group	No. of cases	Predicted group membership	
		Group I	Group II
Group 1 (Low level)	13	69.2%	4 30.8%
Group 2 (High level)	22	27.3%	16 72.7%

Per cent of grouped cases correctly classified : 71.4 per cent.

The above table 6.45 gives the results of the reclassification. The function, using the variables selected in the analysis classified 71.4 per cent of the cases correctly in the respective groups.

It is found from the Multiple Discriminate Function Analysis applied to the respondents based on the low level and high level of women in family decision making that the following factors significantly discriminate the two level groups.

1. Age (at 1 per cent level)
2. Occupation (at 1 per cent level)
3. Income (at 1 per cent level)

Conclusion

From this chapter it can be concluded that the husband dominates in taking final purchase decision for the durable goods in 90 per cent of the respondent's family as his taste is good and has good knowledge about the goods. Factor Analysis extracts two main factors in which male supremacy in family purchase decisions. Women who are self confident and independent take final decision in the purchase of durable goods in only 1/10 of respondent's family. ANOVA shows that there is good association among education, employment and area of residence and women in decision-making.

Multiple regression analysis shows that if there is increase in women's education, occupation, family size and number of children women will have autonomy in family purchase decision-making. According to the findings of the Step-wise Multiple Discriminant analysis age, income and occupation are better predictors for women as regards decision-making power in the family.

Summary of Findings, Suggestions and Conclusion

Introduction

Family is the basic purchasing and consuming unit and is, therefore, of great importance to marketing manager of all the products. Similarly, they are the primary mechanism through whom cultural and social class values and behaviour patterns are passed on to the next generation. Family decision making involves consideration of questions such as who buys, who decides and who uses. It is complex as it involves emotional and interpersonal relations as well as product evaluation and acquisition. Marketing managers must analyse the family decision process separately for each product category within each target market. The participation of family members in the decision process depends on their involvement with the specific product, role specialisation, personal characteristics and lastly culture and sub culture. Thus, a study of this kind will contribute, to a great extent, to this requirement of the marketers in designing the messages for advertisement strategy and to succeed in this competitive world.

Major Findings of the Study

Demographic Factors of the Respondents

The socio-economic characteristics of 355 respondents are that 41.7 per cent of the respondents are above the age 40 and the education level of the respondents shows that 29 per cent are Post Graduates, 27 per cent Undergraduates and 18 per cent Professionals. Most (45 per cent) of the respondents are home makers and 27 per cent among married working women are employed in government sector and 21 per cent in private organisations. The income of their family is evenly distributed at all levels—38 per cent above Rs. 40,000 per month, 36 per cent below Rs. 20,000 per month and 26 per cent between these two income levels.

Regarding religion of the respondents 54 per cent are Christians, 35 per cent Hindus and 11 per cent Muslims. Similarly, community classification shows 87 per cent are Backward Class and 12 per cent Forward Class. With regard to locality, 64 per cent are living in urban area and the remaining in rural area. 66 per cent have a family size of 4-5 members and most of them have only two children (77 per cent). 70 per cent of the respondents have medium wealth *i.e.,* below Rs.20 lakhs and most (74 per cent) of the respondents live in a nuclear family.

Buying Behaviour

Television : The brand 'Sony' leads (30.1 per cent) in the Television industry. 'Onida' is popular among 20 per cent of the respondents and LG among 17 per cent. Thus multi-national companies capture a major share in the Television industry. Regarding type of Television, the ordinary type is preferred by more than half (56 per cent) of the respondents and the flat type by 32 per cent. New types (LCD type) are not popular. 21 inch screen type is owned by majority (55 per cent) of the respondents and 24 inch by 15 per cent. Big size Television is preferred to small screen size of Television.

Refrigerator : The analysis of purchase decision on Refrigerator reveals that majority of the respondents prefers Multinational Companies' products and it occupies a major market share of 31 per cent by Whirlpool and 28.2 per cent by LG. Godrej captures 15.2 per cent, and Kelvinator 8 per cent of the respondents. Similarly, the single door Refrigerator is preferred by 2/3 of the respondents (66 per cent) and the double door by 1/3 (33 per cent). The most sought after size of Refrigerator is 180 litres (39 per cent). Refrigerator with the capacity of 165 litres is chosen by 29 per cent of the respondents. Very big and very small are not preferred by the respondents. Red is the most preferred colour (35 per cent) among the respondents and next preference goes to Grey (25 per cent) colour.

Washing Machine : Regarding Washing Machine Multinational Companies lead in which Whirlpool captures 28 per cent of the respondents, LG 22 per cent and IFB 16 per cent. Videocon captures 15 per cent of the respondents. Majority of the respondents prefers the Front Loading Washing Machine (77 per cent) and the Fully Automatic Washing Machine is preferred (52 per cent) to Semi Automatic ones. The most preferred size of Washing Machine is the 5.5 litres (33 per cent) and the 5 litres by 29 per cent of the respondents. Very big size is not preferred.

Two Wheeler : Only 1/4 of wives (24.2 per cent) own Two Wheelers and the brand they choose is TVS (66 per cent) and 60 CC Two Wheeler (63 per cent). Men prefer Hero Honda (43 per cent). Next preference goes to TVS (28 per cent). 100 CC bikes are their favourite (66 per cent). Very big Two Wheelers are not preferred by husbands. The most sought after colour among both the sex is black (60 per cent wives and 64 per cent husbands). The next preferred colour is Grey (15 per cent) by husbands and Green (12 per cent) by wives.

Regarding the type of ownership of all these durable goods almost all (99 per cent) the respondents prefer brand new ones to second hand ones. Majority of the respondents buy Television (86 per cent) Refrigerator (71 per cent) Washing Machine (64 per cent) and Two Wheelers (58 per cent) from their own savings but purchase of durable goods in instalments is common in case of Two Wheelers (35 per cent) rather than other durable goods.

Regarding replacement behaviour more than half of the respondents (Television 52 per cent, Refrigerator 63 per cent, Washing Machine 56 per cent and Two Wheeler 62 per cent) exchange their old ones for new ones and only a few

(Television 32 per cent, Refrigerator 23 per cent, Washing Machine 22 per cent and Two Wheeler 28 per cent) sell their old durable goods in order to replace.

Process of Family Purchase Decision Making

The process through which the members of the family go through before, during and after making a purchase helps the marketers in planning the marketing strategy. By applying Henry Garrett Ranking technique it is found that durable goods are purchased as it is considered as a 'necessity' for their family for it has got the highest mean score. The next reason is for 'comfort and convenience'. The third reason for buying durable goods is 'to save time'.

The respondents usually prefer to collect information both from social source of friends, family members and colleagues and printed advertisements in newspaper and magazine rather than oral advertisement over Television and Radio for purchasing Television, Refrigerator and Two Wheeler. For Washing Machine they generally collect information from oral advertisement and social sources rather than printed advertisement. Modern technology like Internet advertising, e-mail and mobile advertisement are not preferred by women respondents.

To know the inducement factors for selecting brands Henry's Garrett Ranking technique is employed. In general Advertisement plays a very important role for evaluating the brands for all the selected durable goods. In addition, 'friends and relatives' are the main inducing factors for Television and Refrigerator. For Washing Machine 'family members' are the main inducement factors. But for Two Wheeler 'past experience' plays an important role.

'Good will' is the main factor considered for the store selection as it has got the highest mean score in Garrett Ranking. The second and third rank are scored for the factors 'Good after sales service' and 'Price offer' offered by retailers. Showroom and less formality in purchase are the least important factors considered for store selection.

Regarding post purchase behaviour the dissatisfied respondents have the habit of taking public action of complaining to stores (53 per cent) and private action of stop buying that brand (53 per cent) and warning friends (46 per cent). The respondents' preference to taking recourse to redressal forum and legal action (2 per cent) is very low which should needs attention.

Factors Influencing the Purchase of Selected Durable Goods

Likerts Summated Five Point Scaling Technique is used to find out the most important factor and least important factor for the purchase of selected durable goods. Similarly, Factor Analysis is used for reducing the factors. Twelve factors of the same kind are used so that a comparative study can be made to understand the factors influencing the purchase of durable goods.

For the purchase of Television, 'performance' and 'durability', 'guarantee' and 'brand name' are the most important factors considered by the respondents. 'Discount offer' and 'neighbours envy' are the least important factors considered. Factor analysis has reduced twelve factors to four factors which are named as 'Product Features', 'Product Functioning', 'Sales Strategy' and 'Brand Equity'.

In the purchase of Refrigerator, 'performance', 'price', 'guarantee' and 'brand name' are the most influential factors and the same factors like Television. 'Discount offer' and 'neighbours envy' are the least influencing factors considered. By using Factor Analysis twelve factors are minimised to three factors having a cumulative percentage of 61.265 and they are named as 'operational influence', 'physical features' and 'external influence'.

For Washing Machine also 'performance', 'guarantee', 'brand name' and 'durability' are the most important factors and 'discount offer' and 'neighbours envy' are the least important factors influencing the purchase by the respondents. Principal Component Analysis extracts five factors which accounts for 59.054 percentages. The factors are 'Fringe benefits', 'brand belief', 'physical features', 'brand image' and 'dealer support'.

For the purchase of Two Wheeler, the most influential factors considered are 'performance', 'price, 'brand name' and 'guarantee' and the least influential factors are 'discount offer and 'neighbours envy'. Factor Analysis has reduced 12 factors into four factors which are named as 'physical features, 'product reliability', 'value equity' and 'emotional influence'.

To conclude performance, guarantee and brand name are the most vital factors considered for the purchase of selected durable goods. Price factor is given more importance only in the case of Refrigerator and Two Wheeler. For all the selected durables 'discount offer' and 'neighbours envy' are given least importance. So these factors should be avoided in the advertisement copy.

This type of analysis helps the marketers in deciding the messages to be conveyed and not to be conveyed in advertisement strategy.

Role of Women in Family Decision Making

As an initiator women play a little role in the purchase of Television and Two Wheeler but for Refrigerator (52 per cent) and Washing Machine (57 per cent) she plays a major role. Joint initiation role is reasonable for all the selected durables. Husband is the main influencer for all the four products. Women, acting as an influencer, is little higher than husbands for Refrigerator and Washing Machine. In motivation role women's autonomy is the highest for Refrigerator (52 per cent) and Washing Machine (45 per cent) while for Television and Two Wheeler, husbands have greater say than wife. Children's motivating power is reasonable for all the durables.

Regarding nurturing habit, men dominate for Television and Two Wheeler and women for Refrigerator (44 per cent) and Washing Machine (51 per cent). Children also exert influence for Television, Refrigerator and Two Wheeler to some extent.

In deciding the time and place of purchase, husband's influencing power is more than the wife. Joint influence is also quite reasonable in deciding the time of purchase of durables and wives empowerment is fairly good in deciding the place of purchase for Refrigerator (30 per cent) and Washing Machine (34 per cent).

Product features of brand, colour, model and size are mainly decided by women for Refrigerator and Washing Machine. For Television and Two Wheeler, these decisions are dominated by the husband. Joint decision is also fairly good for Television, Refrigerator and Washing Machine while for Two Wheeler men dominate as they have fairly good knowledge.

In deciding the mode of purchase, husband dominates for all the selected durables. Joint decision is made regarding mode of purchase in more than 20 per cent of the families. Husband also dominates as a purchaser of these products especially for Television (67 per cent) and Two Wheeler (76 per cent). For Refrigerator (40 per cent) and Washing Machine (43 per cent) joint purchase is made.

As a replacement initiator role the husband has greater say for Television (67 per cent) and Two Wheeler (76 per cent) while for Refrigerator (74 per cent) and Washing Machine (67 per cent) it is the women who dominate. Thus it can be concluded that women dominate in playing an expressive role in family purchase decision for Refrigerator and Washing Machine and the husband dominates as an instrumental role for Refrigerator and Washing Machine.

Association Between Area of Residence and Role of Family Purchase Decisions

The area of residence has also an impact in making the purchase decision. To understand the relationship between the urban and the rural families and the role of members in family purchase decision making chi-square test has been adopted. It is found that there is significant association between the urban and the rural families in this regard initiating role in Washing Machine, and Two Wheeler, influencing role in Washing Machine, time decision in Two Wheeler, place decision in Refrigerator, brand decision in Washing Machine and the role as purchaser in Washing Machine at 99 per cent confidence level.

Similarly, there is association between the area of residence and the decision regarding the brand of Television and Two Wheeler and purchaser role of Refrigerator at .05 significant levels as in these cases the null hypothesis is rejected at 95 per cent confidence level.

Other roles have accepted the null hypothesis at .05 significant levels as the calculated value is less than the table value.

Relationship between Employment and Role of Family Purchase Decision

Employment of women is one of the important factors which change the role of each member in the family while taking family purchase decision of durable goods. In order to find whether there is any significant difference between the families with working women and non-working women in the role of purchase decision making chi-square test has been employed in this study. The results indicate that there is a remarkable relationship at one per cent between place decision of Refrigerator, brand decision of Refrigerator, purchasers of Refrigerator, and the working women and non-working women families.

Similarly, there is significant relationship at 95 per cent confidence level between the initiators of Refrigerator, influence of Television, time decision of Two Wheeler and brand decision of Two Wheeler and the working women and non-working women families as null hypothesis is rejected.

Other roles of family purchase decision have no relationship with the employment of women as null hypothesis is accepted at .05 significant levels.

Final Decision Makers in the Family

In the family, according to the opinions expressed by women the husband usually takes the final purchase decision for the purchase of durable goods in 90 per cent of families and in only 10 per cent of family's women in the family take the final purchase decision of durable goods.

According to the opinion of wives, the husband dominates in the family purchase decision as 'husband's taste is good' and 'husband has good knowledge' about durables as these factors receive the first two ranks by applying Likerts Five Point Scaling Technique.

Factor analysis by using Principal Component Analysis, Varimax and Kaiser Rotation has extracted two factors from 9 variables. They are named as 'Male Chauvinism' and 'Female Inferiority'. In the total variation 'Male Chauvinism' has exhibited 41.799 per cent followed by 'Female Inferiority' 32.499 per cent.

Only in 10 per cent of the respondents 'women' in the family take the final purchase decision. The scaling technique shows that women who are 'self confident' and 'independent' take the final purchase decision as these factors score the first two ranks. Similarly, women who have good knowledge about durable goods and educated women likes to take the final purchase decision.

Socio-economic Factors Influencing Women in Decision Making

Regarding the demographic factors and women as final purchase decision maker, Rural Christian, Backward Class, undergraduate homemakers above the age of 40 who are living in a big family, having family monthly income of less than Rs. 20, 000 and 2 children and whose wealth position is below Rs. 20 lakhs living in a nuclear family have higher autonomy in family purchase decision of durable goods than others.

Analysis of Variance (ANOVA) is applied in order to test

the hypothesis of finding out the relationship between demographic factors and women as family purchase decision makers. The results show that there is considerable association between, education (P<.01), employment (P<.01) and area of residence (P<0.05) of women and women's autonomy in family purchase decision-making. There is no significant relationship between other independent variables of age, income, religion, community, family size, number of children, wealth position and family type and women as family purchase decision makers of durable goods.

The result of Multiple Linear Regression Analysis shows that if there is improvement in women's education, occupation, community, family size and number of children in the family women will be a better decision maker for the purchase of durable goods. Other independent variables such as women's age, family income, area of location and family type will have an inverse reaction of women's autonomy in the purchase decision in their family. The R^2 value is 0.84 and six independent variables of occupation, monthly income, religion, area of location; family size and family type are statistically significant for the prediction of women's autonomy in family purchase decisions.

Step-wise Multiple Discriminant Function Analysis shows that independent variables of women's age, family income and women's employment are the better predictors in women autonomy in family purchase decision than other independent variables.

Problems Faced on the Purchase of Durable Goods

One of the important problems faced by the respondents on the purchase decision of durable goods is marketing problem, where unfair trade practices of 'misleading advertisement' (38.6 per cent) scores over other marketing problems of 'poor after sales service' (21 per cent) and 'providing wrong information' (20 per cent).

'Over maintenance expenses' (22 per cent) is the leading financial problem and 'over investment' (11 per cent), 'unnecessary payment of interest' (10 per cent) and 'unnecessary investment' (10 per cent) are the other less important financial problems faced by the respondents.

Among the mental problems faced by the respondents 'decision without enquiry' (14 per cent) is the major problem. Purchase of durables is 'not necessary' has been felt by 7 per cent of the respondents.

Marketers should make note of these in order to survive in this competitive world and to earn good will from customers. They should reduce unfair trade practices of misleading advertisement and providing wrong information about goods in the advertisement which will initiate dissatisfaction among people.

Suggestions of the Study

On the basis of the findings of this study, the following suggestions have been made which would help the women gain autonomy in family purchase decisions of durable goods which in turn would help the marketers explore a good marketing and advertising strategy in the sale of durable goods.

To Women

- As 'self confidence' and 'independence' of women are the most important factors essential for the women to have autonomy in family purchase decisions, these should be developed among girls from childhood onwards in Indian families.
- Better knowledge about durable goods would make a dominant decision maker. Women in the family should earn more knowledge about durable goods from various sources of advertising and modern technology and strive to learn more about durable goods to be an excellent family decision maker.
- Education and employment of women have a significant impact in the family for a woman to have

good empowerment. This should be developed in order to have autonomy in family purchase decisions.

- Mobilising money is another vital factor to have power in family purchase decisions. This should be developed by women.
- Proper enquiry should be done before purchasing durable goods so that that problem can be resolved.
- Women should develop interest and show involvement in the durable goods to have empowerment in family decision making.

To Marketers

- The advertising message should convey that purchase of durable goods is a necessity for comfort and convenience as these are the main reasons for buying durable goods. The phrase durable goods are an asset should not be displayed in the advertisement copy.
- Misleading advertisements and providing wrong information are the main problems faced by the respondents in the purchase of durable goods. Marketers should try to solve this problem by providing factual and correct information about the product. Otherwise, advertisement which is the main influential factor in the purchase of durable goods will become a 'waste'.
- Customers should be taken care of by the retailers or the manufacturers by attending to their complaints regarding the products purchased. Otherwise, the customers would take to private means of warning friends or brand swifting behaviour which will affect the goodwill of the manufacturer who may in due course loose existing customers. So complaining behaviour should be welcomed.
- Purchase of durable goods on instalment basis is not popular among the respondents except for Two

Wheelers. So retailers should offer attractive deals and schemes in order to encourage instalment buying of durable goods.

- Modern technology of Internet, email, SMS advertising are not popular among the respondents which should be encouraged among women.
- Poor after sales service is an important marketing problem faced by the respondents. Marketers should give good and effective after sales service as it is one of the important criteria for selecting a store for the purchase of durable goods.
- Advertisement for Television and Two Wheeler should be directed to husband as he plays a dominant role in the purchase of these goods and for Refrigerator and Washing Machine it should be directed to women of the family as she plays a dominant role.
- Long time guarantee and warrantee should be given for durable goods so that maintenance cost of these goods can be reduced.
- Price offer facility and more choice of brands are some of the vital factors considered by the respondents in selecting the stores. So retailers should have wide variety of goods and often give price offer facility in order to attract customers.
- Showrooms are not preferred by the respondents as there will not be variety of brands of goods available. Respondents feel that choice of brands is a criterion for store selection.
- Advertisement, especially Television advertisement, plays a great role in providing information about the durable goods. So manufacturers should take this fact into account before deciding on the advertising strategy.
- While designing advertisement message importance should be given to factors like performance, brand

name and guarantee as these are the vital factors considered for the purchase of durable goods. At the same time, messages conveying about discount and neighbours envy should be avoided as they are least important factors considered in the purchase of durable goods.

- Indian companies should produce good quality durable goods at reasonable price to compete with Multinational Companies, which now dominates the market of durable goods.
- As purchase of second hand durable goods is not popular, the people have the habit of exchanging old ones for new goods. But this will cause waste as maximum yield on goods are not utilised. So purchasing second hand goods should be encouraged.
- Only very few percentage of the respondents is seeking the government's redressal forum in case of dissatisfaction. Government should take steps to make awareness of consumerism so that they can get the maximum benefit out of it.
- The respondents prefer medium size Television (21"), Refrigerator (180 litres), Washing Machine (5.5 litres) and Two Wheeler (100 CC). Accordingly, the manufacturer should concentrate on producing the goods taking into consideration size and colour preferred by the respondents.
- For Two Wheeler and Television oral advertising plays an important role but for Refrigerator and Washing Machine printing advertisement plays a good role which should be given attention to.

Conclusion

The present study has brought to light the women factor in family purchase decisions of durable goods. 'Women' in the family play a dominant expressive role in the purchase of Refrigerator and Washing Machine as they are more involved in these two products and husbands dominate in the purchase of Television and Two Wheeler, playing an instrumental role for Refrigerator and Washing Machine. Husbands in 90 per cent of the respondent's family take the final decision regarding the purchase as he has good taste and knowledge about the products and not because of their masculine nature which has been admitted by the wives. Women who are "self confident and independent" show greater autonomy than men in family purchase decision. Similarly, income, education and employment of women have an impact on family decision making. The researcher has specifically made important suggestions for the improvement of women in family decision-making. If the said suggestions are considered by women and marketers both can succeed in their respective fields.

Moreover, the present study will induce the researchers of marketers to probe further in this field. The researcher, from personal experience, has advocated the following issues for further research.

(*i*) A study on the adolescents' influence in family purchase decision.

(*ii*) A study on the role of family members in the purchase of non-durable goods (FMCG)

(*iii*) A comparative study on the role of women in family purchase decision of durable and non-durable goods.

Bibliography

Books

Assael Henry., *Consumer Behaviour—A Strategic Approach*, New Delhi, Biztantra, An Imprint of Dreamtech Press, 2005.

Assael Henry., *Consumer Behaviour and Marketing Action*, New Delhi, Replika Press Pvt. Ltd., 2001.

Beri, G.C., *Business Statistics*, New Delhi, Tata McGraw Hill Publishing Company Limited, 2006.

Berkman W. Harold, et al., *Consumer Behaviour—Concepts and Strategies*, Berkman, Kent Publishing Co., 1986.

Cundiff W. Edward et al., *Fundamentals of Modern Marketing*, New Delhi, Prentice Hall of India Pvt. Ltd., 1982.

David Loudon L. et al., *Consumer Behaviour*, McGraw Hill, Inc, New Delhi, 1983.

Engel F. James, et al., *Consumer Behaviour*, Illinois, The Dryden Press Hinsdate, 1978.

Gandhi, J.C., *Marketing—A Managerial Introduction*, New Delhi, Tata McGraw Hill Publishing Company Limited, 1989.

Hawkins I. Del et al., *Consumer Behaviour Building Marketing Strategy*, New Delhi, Tata McGraw Hill Publishing Company Limited, 2007.

Jain P.C. et al., *Consumer Behaviour in Indian Context*, New Delhi, S. Chand and Company Ltd., 2003.

Kotler Philip, *Marketing Management*, New Delhi, Prentice Hall of India Pvt. Ltd., 1988.

Lindquist D. Jay, et al., *Shopper, Buyer and Consumer Behaviour*, New Delhi, Biztantra, An Imprint of Dreamtech Press, 2006.

Loudon L. David et al., *Consumer Behaviour Concepts and Applications*, New Delhi, McGraw Hill, Inc., 1993.

Mamoria, C.B., et al., *Marketing Management*, Allahabad, Kitab Mahal, 1991.

Nargundkar Rajendra, *Marketing Research Text and Cases*, New Delhi, Tata McGraw Hill Publishing Company Limited, 2008.

Neelamegham, S., *Marketing in India—Cases and Readings*, New Delhi, Vikas Publishing House Pvt. Ltd., 2004.

Patawain Swapna, *Women Managers*, Jaipur, RBSA Publishers, 2006.

Raju, M.S., et al., *Consumer Behaviour, Concepts, Applications and Cases*, New Delhi, Vikas Publishing House Pvt. Ltd., 2005.

Redman J. Barbara, *Consumer Behaviour—Theory and Application*, Connecticut, AVI Publishing Co., Inc., 1979.

Reynolds D. Fred, et al., *Consumer Behaviour*, New York, McGraw Hill Book Co., 1977.

Schiffman G. Leon et al., *Consumer Behavior*, New Delhi, Prentice Hall of India Private Limited, 2005.

Sherlekar, S.A., *Marketing Management*, Bombay, Himalaya Publishing House, 1986.

Sinha Kumar Ajit., *New Dimensions of Women Empowerment*, New Delhi, Deep and Deep Publications Pvt. Ltd., 2008.

Stanton William J., *Fundamentals of Marketing*, Singapore, McGraw Hill International Book Company, 1981.

Woodruff, et al., *Marketing Management*, New Delhi, Laxman Chand Arya, 1988.

Journals

Allen Elizabeth Sandin, et al., "Decision-Making Power, Autonomy and Communication in Remarried Spouses Compared with First-Married Spouses", *Family Relations*, Vol.50, No.4, 2001.

Anderson Rolph E., "Consumer Dissatisfaction; The Effect of Discontinued Expectancy on Perceived Product Performance", *Journal of Marketing Research*, Vol.11, No.1, (February 1973).

Aribara Anocha, et al., "Understanding the Role of Preference Revision and Concession in Group Decisions", *Journal of Marketing Research*, Vol. XXXIX, No. 3, August 2002.

Arora Neeraj and Allenby Greg M., "Measuring the Influence of Individual Preference Structures in Group Decision Making", *Journal of Marketing Research*, Vol. XXXVI, No. 4, November 1999.

Atkin Charles K., "Observation of Parent Child Interaction in Supermarket Decision Making", *Journal of Marketing*, Vol. 42, No. 4, October 1978.

Bajpai Suman, "Women is Becoming Techno-Smart", *Woman's Era*, Vol. 35, No. 828, June (first) 2008.

Barach Jeffrey, A., "Consumer Decision Making and Self Confidence", *Indian Journal of Marketing*, Vol. 2, No. 3, September 1971.

Bayus Barry L. and Mehta Raj, "A Segmentation Model for the Targeted Marketing of Consumer Durables", *Journal of Marketing Research*, Vol. XXXII, No. 4, November 1995.

Berey Lewis A., and Pollay Richard W., "The Influencing Role of the Child in Family Decision Making", *Journal of Marketing Research*, Vol. 5, February, 1968.

Bryant Keith W., "Durables and Wives' Employment Yet Again" *Journal of Consumer Research*, Vol. 15, No. 1, June 1988.

Burns Alvin C. and Granbois Donald H., "Factors Moderating the Resolutions of Preference Conflict in Family Automobile Purchasing", *Journal of Marketing Research*, Vol. XIV, No. 1, February 1977.

Carlson Les and Grossbart Sanford, "Parental Style and Consumer Socialisation of Children", *Journal of Consumer Research*, Vol. 15, June 1988.

Chief Educational Officer, Nagercoil and District Elementary Educational Officer, Nagercoil, cited in District Statistical Hand Book 2006-07.

Corfman Kim P., and Lehmann Donald R., "Models of Co-operative Group Decision Making and Relative Influence: An Experimental Investigation of Family Purchase Decision", *Journal of Consumer Research*, Vol. 14, No. 1, June 1987.

Courtney Alice E. and Lockeretz Sarah Wernick, "A Woman's Place: An Analysis of the Roles Portrayed by Women in Magazine Advertisements", *Journal of Marketing Research*, Vol. 8, No. 1, February 1971.

Cox Eli P., "Family Purchase Decision Making and the Process of Adjustment", *Journal of Marketing Research*, Vol. XII, No. 2, May 1975.

Cunningham Isabella C.N., and Green Robert T., "Purchasing Roles in the U.S. Family 1955 and 1973", *Journal of Marketing*, Vol. 38, No. 4, October 1974.

Curry David J., and Menasco Michael B., "Some Effects of Differing Information Processing Strategies on Husband-Wife Joint Decisions", *Journal of Consumer Research*, Vol. 6, No. 2, September 1979.

Curry David J., and Menasco Michael B., "Utility and Choice: An Empirical Study of Wife/Husband Decision Making", *Journal of Consumer Research*, Vol. 16, No. 1, June 1989.

Davis Harry L., "Decision Making Within the Household ", *Journal of Consumer Research*, Vol. 2, No. 4, March 1976.

Davis Harry L., "Dimensions of Marital Roles in Consumer Decision Making", *Journal of Marketing Research*, Vol. VII, No. 2, May 1970.

Davis Harry L., "Measurement of Husband-Wife Influence in Consumer Purchase Decisions", *Journal of Marketing Research*, Vol. VIII, No. 3, August 1971.

Davis Harry L., and Rigaux Benny P., "Perception of Marital Roles in Decision Processes", *Journal of Consumer Research*, Vol. 1, No. 1, June 1974.

Filiatrault Pierre and Ritchie Brent, J.R., "Joint Purchasing Decisions: A Comparison of Influence Structure in Family and Couple Decision Making Units", *Journal of Consumer Research*, Vol. 7, No. 2, September 1980.

Foxman Ellen, et al., "Adolescents Influence in Family Purchase Decisions; A Socialisation Perspective", *Journal of Business Research*, Vol. 18 (Second Issue), 1989.

Foxman Ellen, et al., "Family Member's Perceptions of Adolescents' Influence in Family Decision Making', *Journal of Consumer Research*, Vol. 15, No. 4, March 1989.

Fry Joseph N., and Siller Fredrick H., "A Comparison of Housewife Decision Making in Two Social Classes", *Journal of Marketing Research*, Vol. VII, No. 3, August 1970.

Green Robert T. and Cunningham Isabella, C.M., "Feminine Role Perception and Family Purchasing Decision", *Journal of Marketing Research*, Vol. XII, No. 3, August 1975.

Greenleaf Eric A., and Lehmann Donald R., "Reasons for Substantial Delay in Decision Making", *Journal of Consumer Research*, Vol. 14, No. 1, June 1987.

Hays S., "Has Online Advertising Finally Grown Up?", *Advertising Age*, April 2002.

Hempel Donald J., "Family Buying Decisions: A Cross Cultural Perspective", *Journal of Marketing Research*, Vol. XI, No. 3, August 1974.

Hill, C.J., "The Nature of Problem Recognition and Search in the Extended Health Care Decision", *Journal of Services Marketing*, Vol. 15, No. 6 (2001).

Isler Leslie, et al., "Children's Purchase Requests and Parental Responses Results from a Dairy Study", *Journal of Advertising Research*, Vol. 27, October/November 1987.

Jejeebhoy Shireen T., "Convergence and Divergence in Spouses Perspectives on Women's Autonomy in Rural India", *Studies in Family Planning*, Vol. 33, No. 4, December 2002.

Jejeebhoy Shireen T., and Sathar Zeba A., "Women's Autonomy in India and Pakistan: The Influence of Religion and Region", *Population and Development Review*, Vol. 27, No. 4, December 2001.

Kasulis et al., "Validating the Retail Store Image Concept", *Journal of Marketing*, Vol. 45, No. 1, (Autumn 1981).

Kim Chankon and Lee Hanjoon, "Development of Family Triadic Measures for Children's Purchase Influence", *Journal of Marketing Research*, Vol. XXXIV, No. 3, August 1997.

Krishnamurthi Lakshman, "The Salience of Relevant Others and its Effect on Individual and Joint Preference: An Experimental Investigation", *Journal of Consumer Research*, Vol. 10, No. 1, June 1983.

Lakshmanasamy, L., "Nash Bargained Household Decisions; Testing the Economic Models of Family in India", *Indian Economic Journal*, Vol. 50, Nos. 3 & 4, 2002-03.

Madhubalan Viswanathan, et al., "Decision Making and Coping of Functionally Illiterate Consumers and Some Implications for Marketing Management", *Journal of Marketing*, Vol. 69, January 2005.

Masan, K., "The Status of Women; Conceptual and Methodological Issues in Demographic Studies", *Sociological Forum* 1 (2).

Menasco Michael B., and Curry David J., "Utility and Choice: An Empirical Study of Wife/Husband Decision Making", *Journal of Consumer Research*, Vol. 16, No. 1, June 1989.

Mittal Vikas, et al., "Attribute Level, Performance, Satisfaction and Behavioral Intentions Over Time", *Journal of Marketing*, Vol. 63, No. 2, April 1999.

Mohanram, A.S., and Mahavi, C., "Product Related Characteristics, Promotion and Marketing Mix are Key Tools in Determining Purchase Behaviour and Purchase Decision by Teenagers – An Empirical Study", *Indian Journal of Marketing*, Vol. XXXVII, No. 2, February 2007.

Moschis George P., "The Role of Family Communication in Consumer Socialisation of Children and Adolescents", *Journal of Consumer Research*, Vol. 11, March 1985.

Munsinger Gary M., et al., "Joint Home Purchasing Decisions by Husbands and Wives", *Journal of Consumer Research*, Vol. 1, No. 4, March 1975.

Newman Joseph W., and Staelin Richard, "Pre Purchase Information Seeking for New Cars and Major Household Appliances", *Journal of Marketing Research*, Vol. IX, No. 3, August 1972.

Newman Joseph W., and Werbel Richard A., "Multivariate Analysis of Brand Loyalty for Major Household Appliances", *Journal of Marketing Research*, Vol. X, No. 4, November 1973.

Newman Joseph, W., et al., IMR, Vol.IX, No. 3, August 1972.

Palan Kay N., and Wilkes Robert E., "Adolescent-Parent Interaction in Family Decision Making", *Journal of Consumer Research*, Vol. 24, September 1997.

Park Whan, C., "Joint Decisions in Home Purchasing: A Muddling-Through Process", *Journal of Consumer Research*, Vol. 9, No. 2, September 1982.

Punj Girish N., and Staelin Richard, "A Model of Consumer Search Behavior for New Automobiles", *Journal of Consumer Research*, Vol. 9, No. 4, 8 March 1983.

Qualls William J., "Household Decision Behaviour: The Impact of Husbands' and Wives' Sex Role Orientation", *Journal of Consumer Research*, Vol. 14, No. 4, September 1987.

Rajdeep Grewal, et al., "The Timing of Repeat Purchases of Consumer Durable Goods; The Role of Functional Bases of Consumer Attitudes", *Journal of Marketing Research*, Vol. XLI, No. 1, February 2004.

Ramu, G.N., "Wife's Economic Status and Marital Power: A Case of Single and Dual Earner Couples", *Sociological Bulletin*, Vol. 37 (182), March-September 1988.

Reilly Michael D., "Working Wives and Convenience Consumption", *Journal of Consumer Research*, Vol. 8, No. 4, March 1982.

Richins Marsha, "Negative Word of Mouth by Dissatisfied Consumers – A Pilot Study", *Journal of Marketing*, Vol.47, No. 1, Winter 1983.

Scanzoni John, "Changing Sex Roles and Emerging Directions in Family Decision Making", *Journal of Consumer Research*, Vol. 4, No. 3, December 1977.

Schaninger Charles M., and Allen Chris T., "Wife's Occupational Status as a Consumer Behaviour Construct", *Journal of Consumer Research*, Vol. 8, No. 2, September 81.

Shivakumar, K., and Ravindran, R., "Role of Husband and Wife in Purchase Decisions", *Facts For You*, Vol. 23, No. 8, May 2003.

Shuptrine, F.K., and Samuelson, G., "Dimensions of Marital Roles in Consumer Decision Making: Revisited", *Journal of Marketing Research*, Vol. XIII, No. 1, February 1976.

Singh J., "A Topology of Consumer Dissatisfaction Response Styles", *Journal of Retailing*, Spring 1990, pp. 57-97, cited in Del Hawkins et al., CB., New Delhi, Tata McGraw.

Singh Jagdip, "Consumer Complaint Intentions and Behaviour; Definition and Taxonomical Issues", *Journal of Marketing*, Vol. 5, No. 1, (January 1988).

Singh Raghbir and Kaur Pavleen, "Do Rural and Urban Families Decide Differently to Buy?", *The ICFAI Journal of Marketing Management*, August 2004.

Slama Mark E., et al., "Selected Socio-economic and Demographic Characteristics Associated with Purchasing Involvement", *Journal of Marketing*, Vol. 49, No. 1, Winter 1985.

Spiro Rasann L., "Persuasion in Family Decision Making", *Journal of Consumer Research*, Vol. 9, March 1983.

Su Chenting, et al., "A Temporal Dynamic Model of Spousal Family Purchase-Decision Behaviour", *Journal of Marketing Research*, Vol. XL, No. 3, August 2003.

Verma Renu, "Microfinance and Empowerment of Rural Women", *Kurukshetra*, Vol. 56, No. 11, September 2008.

Vincent Nithila, "A Study on Brand Consciousness among Children and its Effect on Family Buying Behaviour in Bangalore City", *Indian Journal of Marketing*, Vol. XXXVI, No. 1, January 2006.

Ward Scott and Wackman Daniel B., "Children's Purchase Influence Attempts and Parental Yielding", *Journal of Marketing Research*, Vol. 9, August 1972.

Weinberg Charles B. and Winer Russell S., "Working Wives and Major Family Expenditures: Replication and Extension", *Journal of Consumer Research*, Vol. 10, No. 2, September 1983.

Westbrook Robert A., Newman Joseph and Taylor James R., "Satisfaction/ Dissatisfaction in the Purchase Decision Process", *Journal of Marketing*, Vol. 43, No. 4, October 1978.

Websites

http://www.kanyakumari.tn.nic.in/sth-2006.pdf.

http://www.journals.uchicago.edu/toc/jer/current

http://www.marketingpower.com

http://indianjournalofmarketing.com

http://jstor.org/journals/002222437.html

http://en.wikipedia.org/wiki/durablegoods.

Index

A

Abdul Kalam, A.P.J., 4

ANOVA, 17, 32, 131, 136, 163, 172

Availability of spare parts, 93

B

Bajpai, 3

Brand Equity, 168

Buying behaviour of durable goods, 62-103

age, 63

analysis of branch choice, 69-71

brand of two wheelers of respondents, 79-80

– – washing machine, 76-77

buying behaviour, 71-72

– – in two wheelers, 78

capacity preference for wives two wheeler, 80-81

caste, 65-66

colour choice of two wheelers, 81

– of refrigerator, 75

door of washing machine, 77

education, 63-64

effects on consumer dissatisfaction, 101-102

evaluating brands, 86-88

factor analysis, 91-99

factors influencing the purchase decision of selected durable goods, 88-90

husband choice for two wheeler as regards its capacity, 80

– – of brand of two wheeler, 79

introduction, 62

loyalty of respondents, 66

mode of purchase of the durable goods, 82

monthly family income, 64-65

number of children, 67

occupation, 64

ownership of durable goods, 68-69

– – two wheeler, 78-79

problems faced in purchase decision of durable goods, 100-101

process of family purchase decision, 84

profile of sample respondents, 62

reason for store selection, 99-100

reasons for buying durable goods, 84-85

religion, 65

replacements of products, 83

size of refrigerator, 75-76

– – the family, 66
– – washing machine, 78
sources of searching information, 85-86
type of family, 67-68
– – purchase of selected durable goods, 81-82
– – refrigerator door, 74-75
– – washing machine, 77-78
– – television, 72-73
wealth position, 67

C

Christians, 65, 144
Comfort and Convenience, 84
Comparative study
between working women and non-working women, 123-124
brand decision, 120-121, 127-128
influencers, 117-118, 124-125
initiators, 116-117
place of purchase decision, 119-120, 126-127
purchaser, 128-129
– of durable goods, 121-122
relationship between urban and rural families and the role of family purchase decisions, 116
test of significance, 122-123, 129-130
time of purchase, 118-119
– – purchase decision, 125-126
Consumer decision making, 43-61
alternative evaluation and selection, 50-51
consumer decision making process, 43-45
dissatisfaction responses, 59-60
evaluating alternatives, 52-54
evaluative criteria, 51
information search, 49
– – on the internet, 50
introduction, 43
kinds of decision making, 45
extended decision making, 46
limited decision making, 45-46
normal decision making, 45
nature of problem recognition, 46-47
outlet image, 55
– selection, 55
paying for the purchase, 56
post purchase consumer behaviour, 56-57
– – dissonance, 57-58
– – evaluation, 59
process of problem recognition, 47
product disposition, 58-59
purchase, 54
types of purchase situations, 54
– of durable goods and decision making, 46
reducing the range of alternatives, 51-52
result of problem recognition, 49
store loyalty, 55-56
types of information search, 49-50

– – problems recognition, 47-48

E

EPSON, 71

F

Final decision makers in the family purchase of durable goods, 131-163

age and purchase decision made by women, 137-138

area of residence, 147-149

community and women decision makers, 145-147

demographic factors and women in decision making, 136

education and purchase decision made by women, 138-140

factor analysis, 133-135

factors influencing the dominance of women in family purchase decision-making, 135-136

family size and women in decision-making, 149-150

– type and women as decision-maker, 153-155

introduction, 131

monthly family income and purchase decision of women, 142-144

multiple discriminant analysis for the women level in decision making, 159-162

– – functional analysis, 157-159

– regression analysis, 155-157

number of children and women power in decision-making, 150-152

occupation and women in family decision making, 140-142

purchase decision make by women, 135

– – makers in the family, 131-132

relative discriminating index, 162-163

religion and women in purchase decision, 144-145

respondents opinion against husband domination in purchase decision, 132-133

wealth position of the family and women as a purchase decision maker, 152-153

H

Henry Garrett Ranking Principle, 84

Henry Garrett Ranking Technique, 16

Henry Garrett Ranking, 167

Hindus, 65, 144

I

Introduction, 1-23, 164

limitations of the study, 19-20

methodology, 14

need for the study, 9-10

null hypothesis defined, 12

objectives of the study, 12

operational definitions, 12

autonomy, 12

durable goods, 13

empower, 13

extended family, 13

family, 13
– decision making, 13
– purchase decisions, 13
nuclear family, 13
selected durables, 13
women, 14
period of study, 19
roles of family members in the family decision making process, 4-9
scope of the study, 11-12
statement of the problem, 10-11

K

KMO, 91, 133

L

LG, 74
Likert Five Point Scaling Technique, 135
Likerts Summated Five Point Scaling Technique, 168

M

Major findings, 164
association between area of residence and role of family purchase decision, 170-171
buying behavior, 165-167
demographic factors of the respondents, 164-165
factors influencing the purchase of selected durable goods, 168-169
final decision makers in the family, 172
problems faced on the purchase of durable goods, 173-174
process of family purchase decision making, 167-168
relationship between employment and role of family purchase decision, 171
role of women in family decision making, 169-170
socio-economic factors influencing women in decision making, 172-173
suggestions, 174
to marketers, 175-177
– women, 174-175
Male Chauvinism, 135, 172
Multi discriminant analysis, 19
Multinational companies excel, 71
Multiple Discriminant Function analysis (MDFA), 158, 159
Multiple Linear Regression Analysis, 131
Multiple Regression Model, 18
Muslims, 65, 144

N

Nash, 35
Necessity, 84
NGO, 3
Non-Probability Convenient Sampling Technique, 15

P

Principal component analysis, 16, 91, 172
Product features, 168
Product functioning, 168

R

Review of literature, 24-42

Allen, 30, 34
Aribara, 35
Arora, 34
Atkin, 29
Burns, 28
Chenginth, Su, 36
Courtney, 25
Cunningham, 27, 28
Davis, 24
Davis, 25
Foxman, 33
Hempel, 27
introduction, 24
Kim, 33
Lehmann, 32
Mohanram, 37
Park, 31
Qualls, 32
Ramu, 32
Rigauz, 26
Scanzoni, 29
Shivakumar, 36
Shuptrine, 28
Siller, 25
Singh, Raghbir, 36
Staelin, 26
Viswanathan, 37
Ward, 26

Role of women in the decision-making process of family purchase, 104-130
brand of purchase, 109-110
colour of durables, 110-111
comparative study, 116
influences, 105-106
initiator, 104-105
introduction, 104
mode of purchase, 113
model of durables, 111-112
motivator, 106-106
nurturer, 107
place of purchase, 108-109
purchaser of a product, 114
replacement initiator, 114-115
role of women in family purchase decision of selected durable goods, 115-116
size of the durables, 112-113
time of purchase, 108

Rotated component matrix, 92
Rotated factor matrix, 17

S

Sales Strategy, 95, 168
SMS, 176
Suggestions, 164-178

T

Timing of repeat purchases of consumer durable goods, 36
To save time, 84
Two wheelers, 79-80

W

Washing machine, 76-77
Women Empowerment Project, 3

❑❑❑